The Book of the
GRANGE 4-6-0s

By
Ian Sixsmith

Richard Derry

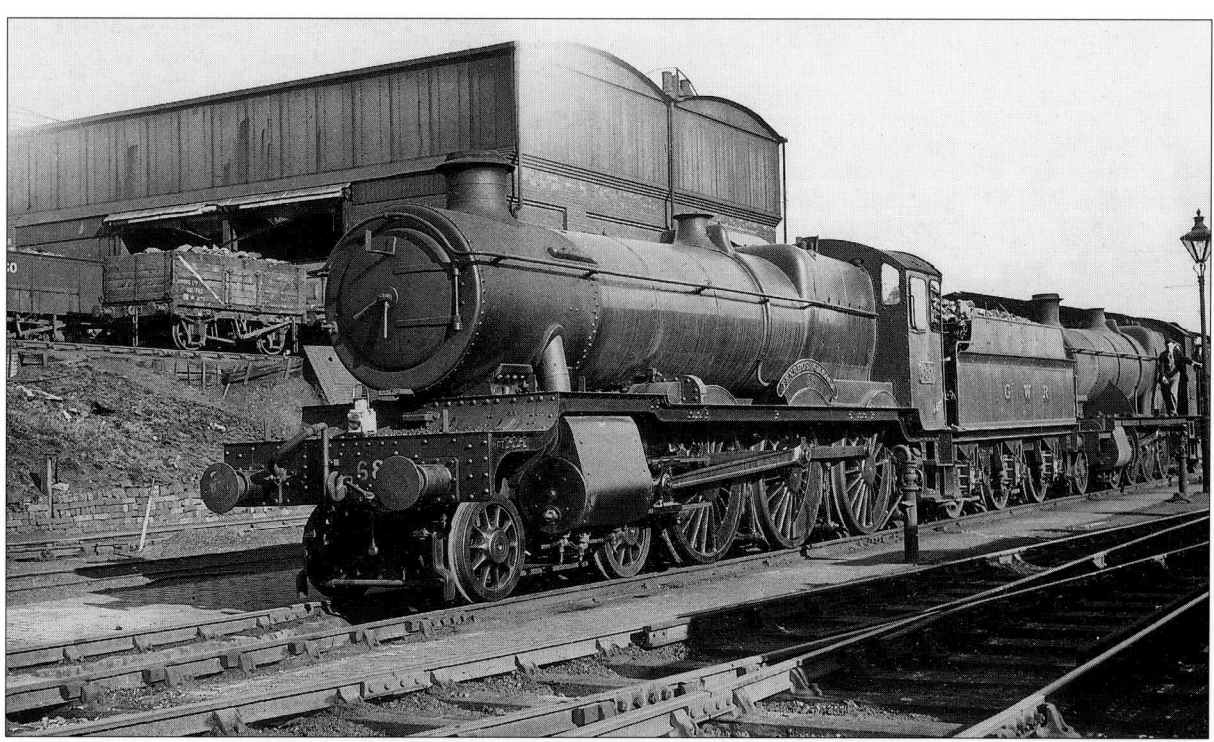

A slightly travel-stained 6868 PENRHOS GRANGE, in plain green, at its home shed Ebbw Junction (it had gone there new) on 4 April 1948; tender now carries the serif GWR. It is *just* possible (on the original anyway) to make out the GWR shed code stencilled behind the buffer beam, the NPT of Newport Ebbw Junction.

Irwell Press Ltd.

Copyright IRWELL PRESS LIMITED
ISBN 978-1-906919-68-9
First published in the United Kingdom in 2014
by Irwell Press Limited, 59A, High Street, Clophill,
Bedfordshire MK45 4BE
Printed by
T. J. International
Padstow, Cornwall.

Acknowledgements

It was Mr Richard Derry of Minehead who once again undertook the task of compiling the tables; an epic undertaking deserving the status of near-deity in Engine Picking circles. As I declared in *The Book of the County 4-6-0s* it should be arranged for an Engine History Card to be incorporated into his family coat of arms.

Equally deserving of praise is Dave Walker; he it was who painstakingly recorded the entries, at the National Archives, photographing them at the dawn of the Digital Age so that we can re-commit them now to good old traditional print.

A corrective rod, its gentle strokes made alternately of admonishment and pity, was applied chiefly, as so often, by Eric Youldon. Other rod wielders include Tony Wright, Edward Chaplin, Richard Woodley, Chris Hawkins, Rob Kinsey, George Reeve, John Hodge, Brian Bailey, Brian Penney, John Nicholas and Mike King.

Contents

New Locos for Old   Page 5
The Record   Page 17

6809 BURGHCLERE GRANGE, built September 1936, at its first shed, Old Oak Common, on 26 March 1937. There was a clutch of Granges at Old Oak from new but (especially post-war) they were not particularly London Division engines – rather after the fashion of the Counties (see *The Book of the County 4-6-0s*). B.K.B. Green Collection, Initial Photographics.

6800 ARLINGTON GRANGE at Swindon early on with Swindon Works curiously faded out by the photographer's art. The first two or three had the freakish cast iron chimneys and painted safety valve covers but fortunately they soon looked like this. The Granges had conventional gravity sanding, to the front of the leading driver and to the rear of the trailing one. The rear sandbox and filler was mounted under the cab, the front one hidden away behind the slidebars; its filler cap sat on the top surface of the running plate and is difficult to spot. The tender is the first type to run with the Granges, low-sided with 3,500 gallons of water; remarkably, they carried seven tons of coal. Unlike the other tenders used with the Granges the cutaway at the front began lower than the bottom of the cab window; the top edge (the 'rave' or 'fender') is in line with the middle of the cab window. They were 10-20 years old (or more) when attached to the new locos. The fact is, tenders lasted longer than locos, at least on the GWR. In these 'official' portraits all manner of details stand out, almost unnaturally so and that was the purpose after all. Take for instance the horizontal 'rodding' gear above the top slide bar: the engines had inside Stephenson Link motion with rocking shafts, to transfer movement from inside to outside. What we see is the valve rod, which connects the valve spindle crosshead to the rocking shaft, the latter transferring the movement of the extension, or intermediate, valve rod from the inside motion to the outside valve. The same arrangement applies on the right-hand side but the valve rod was hidden behind the vacuum pump.

Introduction
New Locos for Old

The second rank of Great Western motive power – the mixed traffic engines if you like – was for years made up of the humble mogul, but this began to come to an end with the widespread use of the new Hall 4-6-0s. The Halls were Saints with wheels reduced from 6ft 8½in to 6ft but most proposals on the GWR went back decades and as far back as the turn of the century, years before even the Halls appeared, a version with even smaller wheels had been mooted. In the 1930s Collett decided to use some of the parts of older 2-6-0s, such as wheels, coupling rods and cab steps, in a class of 80 'different Halls' – a new class called the Granges because of their 5ft 8in driving wheel diameter. The Granges and their smaller brethren, the Manors, were announced at the same time, as 'the engines replacing the 2-6-0s'. The first of these would be 6800-6809 'to be named after Granges' and Manors 7800-7809, though the first of the latter would not appear until 1938.

By late June 1936 the cylinders ('of an improved design') and front ends for 6800-6805 had been assembled in Swindon A Shop. These new cylinders (they were the same for Granges and Manors) at 18½x30 were the same size as those of the moguls but the disposition of the casting meant the 2-6-0 originals could not be utilised – though even if this had been considered this was for the best surely given the years of work they'd already done in 43XXs. Swindon A Shop at this period was busy as usual, with Halls 5962-5965 and pannier tanks 9783-9785 and 7400-7406 building at the time. The frames of 2-6-0s 4331, 4332, 4364 and 4397 were noted loaded on wagons in the dump for disposal. There was a suggestion at first that the Granges/Manors would incorporate the frames of the 43XX engines but this was not so and all the old 43XX and 83XX frames were cut up after reusable 43XX parts were removed in the A shop; it would after all had been asking for trouble (as with the cylinders) to utilise frames that were already a couple of decades old.

The Grange class, it was intended – or at least it was declared at the time – would eventually number 100 engines, though building ceased at eighty with the coming of war. It was also stated, if not at the time then a little later on, that there would have to be some *three hundred* of these new engines, if they were to replace all the 2-6-0s, but war put paid to this too. For both statements to be correct, the GWR intended to build two hundred Manors, which seems unlikely.

The Granges were accounted for as 'conversions' from 43XX 2-6-0s, 'certain usable parts from the old engines being incorporated in the new design' as it was put – though that didn't amount to much, as we've seen above. The principal 'usable part' of course, was the tender which, often enough, had been built even before the 43XX from which the Grange nominally arose. The tender, moreover, simply came from the same pool that was available for the 2-6-0s, not necessarily the specific tender of a nominal 'donor' mogul. The boiler, usefully, was the standard Swindon No.1 as used on the Hall. Almost the only difference from the Hall were those four inches in the driving wheel diameter and the improved cylinders (the Halls, as noted above, had six foot drivers).

6849 WALTON GRANGE brand new at Swindon, 24 October 1937. Shimmering finish to plain green livery; roundel (the 'shirt button') on tender. The light on the new paint also shows how the steampipes were ever so slightly 'jointed' for the No.1 boiler to match the new cylinders; the Manors were the same for the same reason while the Hall steampipes for instance were conventionally straight. There is a small upright object, like an oil bottle on the running plate by the forward splasher. This was the 'class B' vacuum pump lubricator. It supplied oil to the pump cylinder to lubricate the pump piston. They could be seen in the same position on Saints, Halls and Manors too, but they were removed under BR. R.J. Buckley, Initial Photographics.

6877 LLANFAIR GRANGE, a few weeks old on 8 May 1939. The conduit clipped to the side framing carries the wiring to the ATC shoe unit; on Granges the unit was attached to the bogie with the contact shoe carried on a pivot arm. It is fitted so neatly that, if it were possible, you'd feel sure the GW would have found a way of hiding it completely. Holcroft wrote about cleaning up the external lines of Great Western engines, a task with which Churchward specifically charged him. Block lettering of buffer beam number. R.J. Buckley, Initial Photographics.

The principal dimensions were:
Cylinders 18½ x 30in
Driving wheels 5ft 8in
Bogie wheels 3ft
Coupled wheelbase 14ft 9in
Engine wheelbase 27ft 1in
Heating surface in square feet
firebox 154.78
tubes 1,686.60
superheater 262.62
total 2,104
grate area, 27.07
Boiler pressure 225lb
Adhesion weight, 55 tons 3 cwt
Total weight in working order, 74 tons
Tender coal 7 tons, water 3,500 galls
weight, 40 tons
Tractive effort 28,875lb

Motion parts off 43XXs were refurbished and put back, by the look of it, randomly on new Granges or overhauled 43XXs. Some of the parts from 43XXs 'matched' the Grange from which they were nominally converted while – presumably – others didn't.

6800-6803 appeared with cast iron chimneys and painted safety valve covers; the chimney was slightly cartoonish – so insubstantial as to look tapered almost and was wisely done away with. 6804-6809 had copper-capped chimneys and polished safety valve covers and the first four were soon altered to suit. After a few years changes got underway with boilers off Halls and the larger chimneys carried on those duly ran with the Grange concerned. In a similar way interchanged boilers exhibited different levels of superheating.

Tenders
The Granges at first ran with the markedly lower Churchward 3,500 gallon tenders as used with the 43XX 2-6-0s and they frequently appeared with them well into the 1950s, some even in the 1960s. They were the type familiar from use with the Manors and despite their size carried 7 tons of coal. They are obvious of course in photographs; the top of what on the Southern, say, would be called the 'rave' ('fender' seems to have been in use with respect to GWR tenders) came about half way up the cab window; the cutaway began well below it.

By 1960 the majority of Granges were running with Collett 4,000 gallon tenders, the top of the rave being in line with the *top* of the cab window, the cutaway beginning in line with the *bottom* of the cab window. Several had first been noted with these 4,000 gallon tenders (described as 'the larger Hall type tender') during the Second World War. Then others appeared with the high tenders in 1945; these were concentrated in the West and the change was thought to be due to the exacting nature of running between Newton Abbot and Penzance but this turned out to be merely one chance outcome in a random process.

During 1947 more and more Granges were found running with the 4,000 gallon tenders. The trend that developed seemed to be to lose the earlier low tenders but 'reversions' even quite late on were by no means uncommon so the process was protracted. Individual Granges could be observed with low or high-sided tenders; a year or so later each could have changed to the alternate pattern. Great Western tenders are in fact the work of the Devil and any fiendish complication is possible: 6822 ran for about a year in 1948-49 with green 6829's tender and vice versa!

There was yet a third element to the Grange tenders… A small number of high-sided (or at least higher-sided) tenders were built under Collett in 1929-30, nos.2242-2268; originally paired with

6872 CRAWLEY GRANGE at Old Oak Common in 1956; it has the 3,500 gallon 'intermediate' tender in which the cutaway at the front begins *level* with the bottom of the cab window while the top edge (the 'rave' or 'fender') is still in line with the middle of the cab window. As with all Great Western 4-6-0s, there was a lot more going on at the right-hand side than the left. Prominent under the running plate by the front driving wheel is the vacuum pump driven off the crosshead, a more or less standard GWR feature provided in place of a small ejector. Note too, the reversing shaft and the vacuum ejector pipe. Behind the hand rail runs the ejector pipe; hidden beneath that under the cladding are the oil pipes to the cylinders and the Swindon design of smokebox-mounted regulator in the superheater header. The concealed oil piping emerged from the boiler barrel to then enter the smokebox; the dart-shaped cover (where there were stopcocks) above the steampipe is where this piping briefly emerged. Most GW engines had hydrostatic sight feed displacement lubricators mounted in the cab, under the control of the driver. Increased/divided oil supply to valves and pistons meant there was a similar cover on the left-hand side of the smokebox – though not always! (See 6837 FORTHAMPTON GRANGE at Cardiff General.) Michael Boakes Collection.

6838 GOODMOOR GRANGE finished in lined green at Swindon, 11 January 1958. It would leave with another low-sided tender, one that was already over thirty years old. R.F. Smith, transporttreasury.co.uk

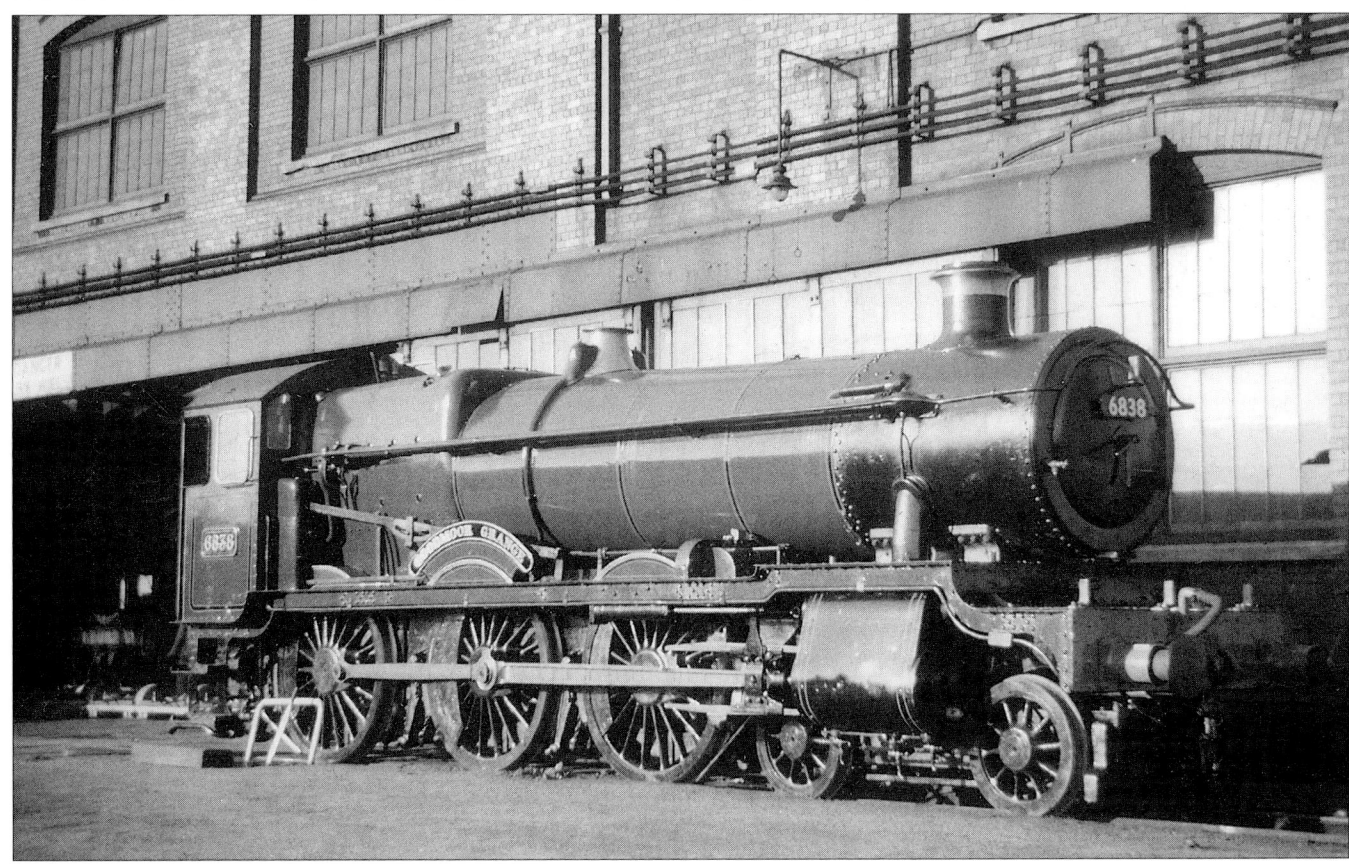

Block lettering on buffer beam on 6852 HEADBOURNE GRANGE (5956 behind) at Newton Abbot, 27 August 1945; 'elbow' (or perhaps we should say 'angle' to avoid confusion with the 'true elbows' of say, the Stars) of steam pipes readily apparent. Policy was that, with rare exceptions, no loco had its 'own' tender, so a change could occur at any works visit or even a shed. There were in fact more tender engines than there were tenders, which was not a problem as it took much longer to repair a loco than a tender. Thus it was unusual for an engine to emerge from overhaul with the tender it arrived with. Churchward favoured a downward tank extension between the frames in the form of a well while Collett preferred a flat bottomed tank flush with the top of the frame. So, for a given capacity the former was lower than the latter with respect to the depth of sides. H.C. Casserley, courtesy R.M. Casserley.

Halls they came to be more closely associated with the Granges. They can usefully be termed 'intermediate' when discussing the Granges. At first glance they look like the familiar 4,000 gallon (6 ton) type that ran behind Halls, Castles, and the rest but they were only of 3,500 gallon and 5½ tons capacity. The top of the 'fender' ('rave' on other railways) was lower than on the 4,000 gallon type and when coupled to a Grange, the rave top was in line with the *middle* of the cab window not the top, making it obviously different from the 4,000 gallon type. As with the 4,000 gallon tenders and unlike the old low-sided ones, the cutaway matched the *bottom* of the cab window.

This 3,500 gallon 'intermediate' type began to be noticed on Granges in 1948-1949 but 6811 seems to have been the first, in 1944. There was official 'word' late in 1952 to the effect that 'all Grange class 4-6-0s are to receive 4,000 gallon tenders' but this of course was never enacted. The general 'trend' was for Granges to acquire 4,000 gallon tenders in place of low-sided 3,500 gallon tenders, running with an 'intermediate' along the way. In fact there was constant change between all three types and only five Granges, 6800, 6847, 6856, 6861 and 6878, never ran with the 'intermediate'.

From 1946 the Hawksworth high sided 4,000 gallon tenders appeared, those specifically for the Counties at 8ft 6in wide and others at 8ft wide which were used almost exclusively on Castles and Halls. These were the latest and final 'standard tender' and were not intended to be used with Granges though they did make brief appearances – with 6853 for a while in 1953 (really just a Swindon Works yard pairing) and 6863 for nearly a year 1953-1954. It was almost inevitable that this convention should break down in the last years and the RCTS *Locomotives of the Great Western Railway* Part 13 notes that 6844 got such a Hawksworth tender (see page 104 for this) in July 1962 and kept it till withdrawal some two years later.

Livery
In the period the Granges were built only express passenger engines got lined GW dark green; along with the Manors they were turned out in plain dark green with the little GWR tender roundel (the 'shirt button') first introduced two years before, in 1934.

From 1942 Granges, like other classes, were outshopped in unlined black. The tender carried GWR in either block or serif.

The emergence of 1000 (see *The Book of the County 4-6-0s*) in 1945 marked the re-appearance of the pre-war GWR lined dark green (officially 'middle chrome green') but with the tender carrying G W with the letters placed either side of the company coat of arms instead of the pre-war shirt button. Green was restored after this, and lining, to Kings and Castles and then some Halls; the Granges remained plain green. In May 1949 6816 FRANKTON GRANGE was probably the first to get the (now BR) unlined black; it would have gone from unlined GW green.

With Nationalisation in 1948 came BRITISH RAILWAYS (or nothing) and in that year 6866 MORFA GRANGE was said to possess the only known low-sided 3,500 gallon tender so titled. A 'W' to indicate 'Western' appeared under cab numberplates on 6842, 6862 and 6866

6807 BIRCHWOOD GRANGE on Filton bank, brand new by the look of it which would make the year 1936. The light load, a 'Bristol Set' suggests 6807 is running in. It would not be the Grange's initial run; that would be light engine with an Inspector and Fitter riding in the cab, a gentle sail to some convenient place. Any adjustments or temporary repairs were carried out once there. 6807 went to Worcester after this, where it stayed all its working life. The neat, joined timber troughing is filled with sand and actually serves as – a sand drag!

6853 MOREHAMPTON GRANGE; this will be later in the 1930s, at what looks to be its home shed Tyseley.

Allocations 1950 and 1959

June 1950

6800 Penzance	6840 St Philips Marsh
6801 Penzance	6841 Banbury
6802 Reading	6842 St Philips Marsh
6803 Banbury	6843 Tyseley
6804 Westbury	6844 Birkenhead
6805 St Philips Marsh	6845 Westbury
6806 Penzance	6846 St Philips Marsh
6807 Worcester	6847 Tyseley
6808 Penzance	6848 Stafford Road
6809 Penzance	6849 St Philips Marsh
6810 Llanelly	6850 St Philips Marsh
6811 St Philips Marsh	6851 Worcester
6812 Stafford Road	6852 St Philips Marsh
6813 Newton Abbot	6853 Tyseley
6814 Newton Abbot	6854 Banbury
6815 Taunton	6855 Laira
6816 Banbury	6856 Oxley
6817 Penzance	6857 Stourbridge
6818 Carmarthen	6858 Tyseley
6819 Birkenhead	6859 Birkenhead
6820 Ebbw Junction	6860 Birkenhead
6821 Ebbw Junction	6861 St Philips Marsh
6822 Newton Abbot	6862 Oxley
6823 Goodwick	6863 St Philips Marsh
6824 Llanelly	6864 Reading
6825 Penzance	6865 Reading
6826 Penzance	6866 Tyseley
6827 St Philips Marsh	6867 St Philips Marsh
6828 Stourbridge	6868 Taunton
6829 Newton Abbot	6869 Penzance
6830 St Philips Marsh	6870 Ebbw Junction
6831 Birkenhead	6871 Severn Tunnel Jct
6832 St Philips Marsh	6872 Truro
6833 Leamington Spa	6873 Laira
6834 Ebbw Junction	6874 Ebbw Junction
6835 Banbury	6875 Pontypool Road
6836 St Philips Marsh	6876 St Philips Marsh
6837 St Philips Marsh	6877 Worcester
6838 Penzance	6878 Birkenhead
6839 Banbury	6879 Oxley

March 1959

6800 Penzance	6840 Pontypool Road
6801 Penzance	6841 St Philips Marsh
6802 Pontypool Road	6842 St Philips Marsh
6803 Stourbridge	6843 Llanelly
6804 St Philips Marsh	6844 Llanelly
6805 Truro	6845 Penzance
6806 Oxley	6846 St Philips Marsh
6807 Worcester	6847 Ebbw Junction
6808 Penzance	6848 Oxford
6809 St Philips Marsh	6849 Laira
6810 Llanelly	6850 Laira
6811 St Philips Marsh	6851 Worcester
6812 Pontypool Road	6852 St Philips Marsh
6813 Newton Abbot	6853 Tyseley
6814 St Blazey	6854 Oxford
6815 Taunton	6855 Truro
6816 Penzance	6856 Worcester
6817 Oxley	6857 Oxley
6818 Llanelly	6858 Oxford
6819 Pontypool Road	6859 Newton Abbot
6820 Worcester	6860 Penzance
6821 Oxford	6861 Tyseley
6822 Oxford	6862 Oxley
6823 Truro	6863 Laira
6824 Penzance	6864 Oxford
6825 Penzance	6865 Ebbw Junction
6826 Penzance	6866 Tyseley
6827 St Philips Marsh	6867 Pontypool Road
6828 Truro	6868 Taunton
6829 Newton Abbot	6869 St Philips Marsh
6830 St Philips Marsh	6870 Penzance
6831 St Philips Marsh	6871 Laira
6832 Truro	6872 Pontypool Road
6833 St Philips Marsh	6873 Laira
6834 St Philips Marsh	6874 Taunton
6835 St Philips Marsh	6875 Penzance
6836 Newton Abbot	6876 St Philips Marsh
6837 Penzance	6877 Worcester
6838 Ebbw Junction	6878 St Philips Marsh
6839 Oxley	6879 Truro

6809 BURGHCLERE GRANGE with an up class H goods, on the bank between Lostwithiel and Bodmin Road, 25 June 1955. R.E. Vincent, transporttreasury

Allocations 1963, 1964 and 1965

February 1963
Banished from the West now; Oxley, Tyseley, Stourbridge just moved to the LMR.

6800 Ebbw Junction	6840 Pontypool Road
6801	6841 Southall
6802	6842 Stourbridge
6803 Oxley	6843 Llanelly
6804 Llanelly	6844 Llanelly
6805	6845 Tyseley
6806 Worcester	6846 St Philips Marsh
6807 Worcester	6847 Cardiff East Dock
6808 Cardiff East Dock	6848 Pontypool Road
6809 Southall	6849 Didcot
6810 Pontypool Road	6850 Ebbw Junction
6811 Stourbridge	6851 Oxley
6812 Reading	6852 Ebbw Junction
6813 Ebbw Junction	6853 Tyseley
6814 St Philips Marsh	6854 Oxley
6815 Llanelly	6855 Oxley
6816 St Philips Marsh	6856 Worcester
6817 Worcester	6857 Oxley
6818 Llanelly	6858 Oxley
6819 Pontypool Road	6859 Cardiff East Dock
6820 Pontypool Road	6860 St Philips Marsh
6821 Pontypool Road	6861 Tyseley
6822 Pontypool Road	6862 Oxley
6823 Oxley	6863 Reading
6824 Didcot	6864 Oxley
6825 Reading	6865
6826 Reading	6866 Tyseley
6827 Stourbridge	6867 Pontypool Road
6828 Oxley	6868 Didcot
6829 Ebbw Junction	6869 Southall
6830 Oxley	6870 Oxley
6831 Oxley	6871 Oxley
6832 Llanelly	6872 Pontypool Road
6833 Oxley	6873 St Philips Marsh
6834 Southall	6874 Didcot
6835 St Philips Marsh	6875 Cardiff East Dock
6836 Pontypool Road	6876 Pontypool Road
6837 Llanelly	6877 Worcester
6838 Pontypool Road	6878 St Philips Marsh
6839 Oxley	6879 Tyseley

October 1964

6800	6840 Llanelly
6801	6841 Oxford
6802	6842 Tyseley
6803 Oxley	6843
6804	6844
6805	6845
6806 Worcester	6846
6807	6847 Cardiff East Dock
6808	6848 Worcester
6809	6849 Oxford
6810 Llanelly	6850 Severn Tunnel Jct
6811	6851 Oxley
6812 Oxford	6852
6813 Worcester	6853 Tyseley
6814	6854 Oxley
6815 Llanelly	6855 Oxley
6816 Barrow Road	6856 Worcester
6817 Worcester	6857 Oxley
6818	6858 Oxley
6819 Worcester	6859 Cardiff East Dock
6820 Cardiff East Dock	6860 Llanelly
6821 Llanelly	6861 Tyseley
6822	6862 Oxley
6823 Oxley	6863 Cardiff East Dock
6824	6864 Oxley
6825	6865
6826 Cardiff East Dock	6866 Tyseley
6827 Oxley	6867
6828	6868 Oxford
6829 Barrow Road	6869 Cardiff East Dock
6830 Oxley	6870 Oxley
6831 Oxley	6871 Oxley
6832	6872 Severn Tunnel Jct
6833 Oxley	6873
6834	6874 Oxford
6835	6875
6836 Worcester	6876 Severn Tunnel Jct
6837 Llanelly	6877 Worcester
6838 Llanelly	6878 Worcester
6839	6879 Tyseley

November 1965

6800	6840
6801	6841
6802	6842
6803	6843
6804	6844
6805	6845
6806	6846
6807	6847 Worcester
6808	6848 Worcester
6809	6849 Oxford
6810	6850
6811	6851
6812	6852
6813	6853 Tyseley
6814	6854
6815 Severn Tunnel Jct	6855 Tyseley
6816	6856 Worcester
6817	6857
6818	6858
6819 Worcester	6859 Severn Tunnel Jct
6820	6860
6821	6861 Tyseley
6822	6862
6823	6863
6824	6864
6825	6865
6826	6866
6827	6867
6828	6868
6829 Worcester	6869
6830	6870
6831 Oxley	6871 Oxley
6832	6872 Worcester
6833 Oxley	6873
6834	6874
6835	6875
6836	6876 Worcester
6837	6877
6838 Worcester	6878
6839	6879 Tyseley

and then smokebox plates. Halls appeared in lined black and the general instruction went out that 4-6-0s and a number of other types should be painted lined black. Of the Granges 6809 and 6819 were so dealt with but no others. The 1st BR emblem, the lion and wheel, began to be applied in 1949.

In 1956 the general instruction as to lined black changed to lined green, with lining on the cylinder covers too; 'all 4-6-0s' were to have the lined dark green though some Granges apparently had managed to acquire it already. The 2nd emblem came in 1957.

1950-53 some had red backgrounds to name/number plates.

Chimneys
Post-war, changes began to be noticed in the chimneys fitted to certain classes as boilers were interchanged; Granges 6810 and 6811, for instance, acquired taller chimneys as fitted to the earlier Halls. As this process went on over the years, almost any chimney could appear on any Standard No.1 boiler. As for capuchons, you takes your pick…

****

The Granges were distributed far and wide and could be found more or less anywhere a 'red' route engine was allowed; it was unsurprising that one, 6802 BAMPTON GRANGE, worked the Oxford to Portsmouth train right through (though it turns out it shouldn't have done) within weeks of entering traffic. Certainly the Great Western started as it meant to go on and the first ten were delivered to give almost every District a taste of the new engines; 6800-6809 went new to Penzance, Laira, Old Oak, St Philips Marsh, Oxley Canton, Landore, Worcester and Penzance. Worcester's new 6807 BIRCHWOOD GRANGE was noted on 15 December 1936, working empty stock in and out of Paddington in between runs back home. The two at Penzance, 6800 and 6809 and Laira's 6801 were making a mark on the main line in Cornwall.

The Granges were good, all round performers, allocated to a large number of sheds, from Birkenhead to Penzance and from Fishguard to Old Oak. They were not allowed over some secondary lines, principally in Mid and North Wales, but were otherwise used extensively. They shared many standard components with the Halls including, as noted, the standard No.1 boiler. The 5ft 8in driving wheels, inherited from the 43XXs, made them quicker getting away than the Halls. The Granges were ideally suited to working their main duties, fast vacuum fitted freights, although they were equally at home on passenger trains, often working express turns. This inevitably changed over the years and by the end of the 1950s the Granges were doing more of the mundane work; weekly mileage was about 600/700.

Brian Penney, some-time contributor to these books as well as to *British Railways Illustrated* magazine, spent time at Worcester in the early 1950s, when the shed had three resident Granges, 6807, 6851, and 6877 and he worked on all three, assisting with mileage exams and routine repairs. He writes: *I was prompted to look up my apprentice log and one entry I noted was for 11th January 1952 when 4086, the booked loco for the 12.15pm London express, became a last minute failure on shed. 6807 was working in with the Hereford portion, due to come off at Shrub Hill, and was remanned by the Worcester top link crew worked the express through to Paddington. At this time 6807 was fitted with a 3,500 gallon tender but managed to complete the working without running out of coal. I spoke to the driver the following day and he said that the loco performed well and they had a right time arrival at Paddington.*

During 1965, the final year of steam on the Western, Worcester had twelve Granges, 28% of the total allocation, and two were still active during the final month before the old place closed. Two, 6807 and 6877, had come new to Worcester and spent all their working lives there. At the beginning of 1965 there were still 43 of the class in service on the Region, which reflected their versatility in being suited to all types of traffic.

Whilst in Swindon Factory I worked on a number of Granges, including the frame Zeissing of 6856 and assisting with the valve setting of 6864. During the final week of my apprenticeship I was on the Trials Gang and went on trial runs with 6839 to Dauntsey. In later years, during my time at Birmingham, Tyseley, Oxley, and Banbury had allocations of Granges, covering a variety of workings. In July the Birmingham Industrial Holiday fortnight took place and a large number of specials were run from the terminus station at Birmingham Moor Street. This station was equipped with a traverser at the dead end to enable locos to be released on to the

6856 STOWE GRANGE at Old Oak in original condition; there was no vacuum pump lubricator by the forward splasher this side for the simple reason there was no vacuum pump this side. W. Hermiston, transporttreasury

adjacent line. Granges were often used on these specials; for example, on 28 July 1961 the midnight express, 1C54 Moor Street to Ilfracombe, was worked by 6862 to Taunton and the 10.15pm, 1C66 Stourbridge to Paignton, was worked by 6841 throughout.

More than twenty Granges were allocated to South Wales sheds and were bought by local scrap merchants after withdrawal. It is remarkable that none was bought by Dai Woodham, with a number of the sheds well within his operating sphere from Barry. Why he went as far as Shrewsbury to buy eight Manors when he could have bought Granges much nearer home, thereby ensuring a preserved example, is a mystery.

6840 HAZELEY GRANGE in black/grime livery, about 1949/50. BR smokebox number plate, as yet no hint of a shed plate, nor the bolts to fix it; GW and the crest still just discernible on the tender. The SPM code (St Philips Marsh) stencilled behind the buffer beam is of interest, for 6840 had only gone there in May 1948, indicating that the old GW codes carried on in use in early BR days. W. Hermiston, transporttreasury

6826 NANNERTH GRANGE, scruffy outside the Old Oak wartime ash shelter, 23 March 1946. H.C. Casserley, courtesy R.M. Casserley.

6848 TODDINGTON GRANGE, in foreign parts at Crewe, 31 May 1947. The original buffers were this tapered variety. H.C. Casserley, courtesy R.M. Casserley.

> **6880 BETTON GRANGE:** *Building the 81st Grange*
> Strangely, though Granges were allocated all around him in South Wales, fate decreed that none would come to Mr Woodham's Barry yard to see eventual salvation. To remedy this glaring omission in the ranks of preserved steam the 6880 Society (a registered charity, No.1100537) was formed in 1998 with the sole intention of recreating a Grange. For information and to make a donation, visit the website at: *www.6880.co.uk*

A filthy 6824 ASHLEY Grange, at the end of the War or soon after, with the plated-over cab window. ColourRail.

Engine Histories

The information herein follows more or less that in the previous 'Book Of' volumes reflecting, largely, what is recorded in the original engine histories, in this case the Swindon Registers and others at The National Archive. This has been married to the record of *The Railway Observer* and other journals. The codes are as follows:

G General
H Heavy
I Intermediate
L Light
R Thought to be 'Running'

The relative frequencies of **L** and **R** indicate they were not recorded with consistency. Also 'Swindon Works' is often noted with no indication as to the level of work done.

WR/BR equivalents after 1948 were:
HC Heavy Casual
HG Heavy General
HI Heavy Intermediate
LC Light Casual
LI Light Intermediate
U Unclassified
C Casual

X/S is thought to stands for 'ex-store'
Cont 'Continuation' – often called 'Rectification' elsewhere. It is a brief recall to works to attend to some minor (or sometimes not so minor) fault showing up after running in following works attention.

Works Dates Compilation of the record from several sources means that dates given of works/outstation shops visits can indicate completion OR beginning of the work. **They thus indicate a period rather than a specific date in or out.**

In some cases not all the information is to hand and 'Mileages and Boilers' might not be represented, say.

With regard to Tenders. For a number of the locos, the sequence of tenders is missing. However in these cases Richard Derry has artfully substituted tender entries as listed in pencil (except where the four figure number is impossible to discern) in the first column for each EVEN year in the GWR/WR shed allocation lists. This will be obvious in the particular table concerned. Sometimes two tenders are listed for a year. The additional entry in square brackets refers to the date of attachment of an 'intermediate' 3,500 gallon tender in the series 2242-2268, information kindly supplied by John Hodge.

As pointed out in other volumes of this series, railway company Engine History Cards, while containing much useful and even fascinating information, are an *indication of* what happened to the engines. A very good and complex indication – the best we will have – but not something that is 100% reliable and accurate in every instance (though it is in many). In the end they were, after all, for Accountants rather than Engineers!

****

An Aside – 'Swindon Targets'

A modified system of controlling the entry of engines into Swindon for heavy repairs was introduced in July 1955. The aim was to provide a more balanced flow of engines of certain types through works, calculated on the numerical strength of each class of engine in each of the nine divisions.

If a high proportion of engines of one type from any single Division required works extra 'pool' engines were needed as cover, beyond what could be accommodated within the Division. The new system was designed to reduce the numbers of any one type in a Division needing works at the same time.

Engines that could be spared in one Division were loaned to make up the shortage of engines in another. This would no longer be necessary.

When a high percentage of engines of one type arrived for heavy repairs together, a shortage of spares – most seriously boilers – could result. The non-availability of a boiler could be the worst cause of prolonged 'waiting' before a loco could complete an overhaul and the new system was intended to alleviate this. It was a most important consideration when admitting engines to works and some margins were worryingly thin. For the nine 47XX 2-8-0s there was one spare boiler, for thirty Counties and Kings five spare boilers each and for thirty Manors only two. For the Castles there were approximately six spare boilers for every thirty-four engines running.

The stock of spare boilers was not based on the number of engines utilising a particular type but was instead determined on the periodicity through works of the engines. This periodicity in turn depended on the types of engines and the duties they were intended to perform. A 2251 0-6-0 led a leisurely life and had a periodicity of forty-six months. A King on the other hand would be expected to appear every sixteen months, or after some seventy thousand miles. The shopping periods (excluding the various ex-LMS types and BR Standards now on the Western Region for which it was responsible) and expected mileages were as (below).

Type	Class	Months	Mileage
4-6-0	60XX	16	70,000
4-6-0	4073	20	80,000
4-6-0	40XX	24	80,000
4-6-0	49XX	30	80,000
4-6-0	68XX	30	80,000
4-6-0	78XX	30	80,000
4-6-0	10XX	20	80,000
4-4-0	90XX	36	70,000
2-8-0	28XX	36	80,000
2-8-0	47XX	-	100,000
2-8-0	30XX	-	60,000
2-6-0	43XX	36	
0-6-0	22XX	46	
0-6-0	23XX	42	
2-8-2T	72XX	42	70,000
2-8-0T	42XX	36	
2-8-0T	5205	36	
2-6-2T	41XX	36	
2-6-2T	61XX	36	
2-6-2T	44XX	24	50,000
0-6-2T	56XX	36	60,000
0-6-2T	RR '30'	42	70,000
0-6-2T	RR '76'	42	70,000
0-6-2T	TV 'O'	40	
0-6-2T	TV 'A'	42	
0-6-0T	57XX	48	80,000
0-6-0T	15XX	48	70,000
0-6-0T	2021	60	70,000
0-6-0T	54XX	42	80,000
0-6-0T	64XX	36	70,000
0-6-0T	74XX	48	80,000
0-6-0T	16XX	48	80,000
0-6-0T	94XX	42	80,000
0-6-0T	'681'	60	70,000
0-4-2T	14XX	48	100,000
0-4-0T	'1142'	60	70,000

The new scheme involved 'target figures' for each of the nine main Divisions within the Western Region: 81A Old Oak Common, 82A Bristol Bath Road, 83A Newton Abbot, 84A Wolverhampton Stafford Road, 85A Worcester, 86A Newport Ebbw Junction, 87A Neath, 88A Cardiff, 89A Oswestry. These tables indicate the number of engines of each type from the various Divisions likely to be found in the works. An engine '½' might seem odd but if the average overall time of repair was, say, four weeks, then it obviously could not be expected that one of the 47XX 2-8-0s would be in works for heavy repair at every visit. 'Allowances made for very good reasons' mean that not all the cross-totals add up. It was also intended that adjustments would become necessary to individual target figures; traffic requirements for instance might result in significant transfers of engines from Division to Division, making for marked alterations to Divisional type totals.

SWINDON FACTORY TARGETS

	DIVISION									
	81	82	83	84	85	86	87	88	89	Total
Class	TARGET									
Kings	1	-	1	1	-	-	-	-	-	3
Castles	3	3	2	2	1	1	1	-	-	13
Counties	-	½	½	½	-	-	½	-	-	2
70000	½	-	½	-	-	½	-	-	-	1
Halls	6	4	3	4	2	2	2	-	-	23
Grange	-	1	2	1	-	½	-	-	-	5
73000	-	½	-	1	-	-	-	-	-	1
75000	-	-	-	-	-	½	-	-	-	1
LMR 5	-	-	-	½	-	-	-	-	-	1
Manors	-	½	1	-	-	-	-	-	-	2
43XX/90XX	2	2	2	5	2	1	1	-	1	16
47XX	½	-	-	-	-	-	-	-	-	1
Totals	13	11	11	15	5	6	5	-	1	67

6800 ARLINGTON GRANGE arriving at Penzance, 22 July 1957. With the eye of faith, the chimney is seen to be taller with no capuchon, an inheritance that came with an improved draughting Hall boiler. Compare with the chimney on say, 6853 on page 9, for instance. The little protruding covers on the curved running plate behind the lamps gave clearance for the dummy glands bolted to the valve chest covers. When the valves were taken out for attention the curved front plates were removed – see 6860 at Worcester for instance, later in the book. In the middle of the curved section, under the smokebox, is the four feed oil box, feeding oil to the tops of the bogie axleboxes from where it was channelled to lubricate the horn faces – on the 2-6-0s there was a two feed oil box, for the two pony truck axleboxes. As well as the little oil 'pot' under the smokebox at the front there were others on the rocker shaft covers – clearly visible here just to the right of the steam pipe. A good view of the ATC shoe – the square component behind that transverse rod. The valve for the steam lance for cleaning the tubes is on left, on the smokebox rim, while the object tucked under the smokebox next to the spare lamp iron, by the steampipe, is the anti-vacuum valve. The curved cover on the running plate above the crosshead conceals the valve rocker for the Stephenson motion. The Grange and Manor cabs were slightly austere; there was no vertical beading to the leading edge. J. Davenport, Initial Photographics.

6800, dull under grime and dirt, at Oxford shed on 17 July 1963. On the 4,000 gallon tender the cutaway at the front, as with the 'intermediate' begins *level* with the bottom of the cab window but the top edge (the 'rave' or 'fender') is in line with the *top* of the cab window. Here endeth the lesson. J.A.C. Kirke, transporttreasury

6800 ARLINGTON GRANGE
Built September 1936

Mileages and Boilers
Date	Mileage	Boiler
9/36		7205
22/9/38	84,044	7205
8/7/40	169,345	7205
24/9/41	211,766	C4424
19/12/42	262,144	C4424
11/9/45	359,249	C2980
10/7/47	437,324	C4054
21/6/50	556,120	C2845
31/3/52	632,521	C2961
23/11/54	752,005	C2961
7/2/57	846,890	C2941
9/5/60	974,509	C2917
28/12/63	1,064,930	C2917

Sheds and Works
15/9/36	Newton Abbot
10/36	Penzance
19/8/38	Swindon Works **I**
30/9/38	Laira
4/6/40	Swindon Works **I**
12/11/42	Swindon Works **I**
4/8/45	Swindon Works **G**
3/47	Landore
10/6/47	Swindon Works **I**
30/10/48	Penzance
19/5/50	Swindon Works **HG**
21/6/50	Penzance
27/2/52	Swindon Works **HG**
10/53	Carmarthen
12/53	Penzance
20/10/54	Swindon Works **HI**
5/1/57	Swindon Works **HG**
26/9/58	Stored
21/3/60	Swindon Works **HG**
14/3/62	Stored
15/6/62	Ebbw Jct.

Tenders
Date	Tender
From new	2125
19/8/38	2204
18/7/41	2026
12/11/42	2906
9/7/45	2872
2/6/44	2008
26/3/49	2039
10/9/49	1985
8/2/50	2077
21/6/50	2015
31/3/52	2866
7/2/57S	2121
2/7/59	2641
9/5/60	2537
?	2719

Mileage as at 28/12/63 1,064,930
Withdrawn 15/6/64 Sold to Birds, Risca 18/8/64

At Ebbw Junction, its last home, 3 September 1964. Peter Groom.

6801 AYLBURTON GRANGE
Built September 1936

Mileages and Boilers
Date	Mileage	Boiler
9/36		7206
4/5/38	88,826	7206
20/2/40	164,539	7206
24/10/42	249,388	C4918
26/1/46	344,156	C2932
14/10/48	444,198	C8256
6/4/51	553,434	C8245
24/8/53	655,698	C4962
17/8/55	741,508	C4962
1/10/57	831,817	C4480

Sheds and Works
19/9/36	Laira
17/3/38	Swindon Works I
26/6/38	Weymouth
15/10/38	Penzance
19/1/39	Newton Abbot Works R
25/8/39	Penzance Shops R
20/2/40	Swindon Works I
4/1940	Newton Abbot
20/8/40	Damaged in air raid at Newton Abbot
24/10/40	Swindon Works R
23/4/41	Newton Abbot Shed R
Sep 1941	Penzance
Oct 1941	Newton Abbot
8/1/42	Newton Abbot Works L
20/8/42	Newton Abbot works R
24/10/42	Swindon Works HG
12/1943	Penzance
11/12/43	Penzance Shops R
17/5/44	Newton Abbot Works L
21/3/45	Penzance Shops R
25/4/45	Penzance Shops L
21/8/45	Newton Abbot Works L
26/1/46	Swindon Works I
13/9/46	Newton Abbot Shops L
6/12/46	Newton Abbot Works L
6/3/47	Penzance Shops R
16/6/47	Newton Abbot Works L
19/9/47	Newton Abbot Works L
21/4/48	Newton Abbot Works L Tender work only
11/8/48	Newton Abbot Works L Tender work only
14/10/48	Swindon Works I
10/10/49	Newton Abbot Works U
27/3/50	Newton Abbot Works U
9/8/50	Penzance Shops U
22/12/50	Penzance Shops U
6/4/51	Swindon Works HI
24/8/53	Swindon Works HG
17/8/55	Newton Abbot Works HI
14/11/56	Penzance Shops U
11/10/57	Swindon Works HG

Tenders
Date	Tender
From new	1986
2/4/38	1728
20/2/40	2003
24/10/42	2898
26/1/46	2876
16/6/47	1983
14/10/48	2258
25/3/50	1819
9/8/52	2577
1/10/57	2748

Final mileage 964,878
Withdrawn 27/10/60, cut up 3/12/60

The Granges did maybe their most memorable passenger work in the West – like 6801 on the down Cornishman near Devonport on 21 April 1954. It was based in Cornwall for almost its entire life and was rarely seen east of Exeter. It was an unlikely victim of air attack – not in Plymouth or London or Bristol or other big centre but in the 'Newton Abbot Blitz' of 1940. It was knocked sideways and though various parts were blown off (though not the nameplate) it stayed upright, unlike pannier 2785 which, memorably, had to be chained to the Grange to prevent it sinking further into the bomb crater! Alan Lathey, transporttreasury

It was well suited to the Cornishman, for it was still on the down train a week later, at Trerule on 27 April 1954. In the meantime someone had arranged for that tender to be cleaned! Alan Lathey, J.A.C. Kirke, transporttreasury

AYLBURTON GRANGE spent its entire working life in the West and all of its BR time at Penzance. Here it is at Laira shed at an unknown date. The filthy tender doesn't help, with no emblem to see, and 6801 had a 4,000 tender from 1952 through to withdrawal. D. Ford, transporttreasury

6802 BAMPTON GRANGE
Built September 1936

Mileages and boilers
9/36		7207
9/7/38	81,428	7207
17/7/40	161,355	7207
3/6/43	262,214	C4428
1/6/47	345,395	C7247
8/2/49	434,123	C8258
19/4/51	503,000	C8233
18/2/54	610,805	C8233
7/2/56	697,240	C2840
19/9/58	810,087	C2840
9/8/61	900,557	C2840

Sheds and Works
17/10/36	Old Oak Common
28/5/38	Swindon Works I
19/8/39	Swindon Works
12/6/40	Swindon Works I
4/1942	Swindon Works
3/4/43	Swindon Works HG
3/1944	Swindon Works
6/1944	Didcot
2/1945	Reading
17/5/46	Swindon Works I
1/11/47	Old Oak Shops
7/12/48	Reading Shops
29/1/49	Swindon Works HI
24/2/51	Swindon Works HG
21/2/53	Laira
18/254	Swindon Works HI
7/2/56	Swindon Works HG
5/10/57	Worcester
2/11/57	Pontypool Road
19/9/58	Caerphilly Works HI

Tenders
From new 2354
17/7/40	1889
11/6/42	2894
2/6/43	1671
5/4/44	2890
1/6/46	1671
21/2/48	2220
8/2/49	2249
29/3/49	2177
19/4/51	1985
18/2/54	2872
7/2/56	2242

Final mileage 900,557
Withdrawn 9/8/61 Cut up 7/10/61

BAMPTON GRANGE at its then home, Laira shed, in 1953; high sided 4,000 gallon tender by now.

To the uninitiated, looking for all the world at first glance a Manor (see below) with a tender like that, 6802 BAMPTON GRANGE stands at Eastleigh with a Southampton Terminus-Reading train on 28 July 1951. Once BR days got under way there were markedly fewer Granges with low tenders. The giveaway to telling a Grange from a Manor (on this side at least) is the ejector pipe under the hand rail; it's absent on the Manors. More generally the Manor chimney is often different with a distinct 'waist' though this is not always so and angles and light can deceive... The carriages (details courtesy Mike King and marvellous to behold behind a GW loco) consist of a rebuilt 58ft LSWR third on SR underframe, followed by an LSWR 3-Lav set, one of those completely formed of 56ft stock with hinged guards doors indicating it to be an ex-4 coach 'cross country' set with LSWR 3-Lav set at the rear – one of those with a single pair of sliding guards doors and the centre coach, also rebuilt on a 58ft SR frame; the whole lot in green. No wonder he writes (excellent) books about them! (A quick way to tell a 68 from a 78 is to glance at the running plate. The Grange has the usual Swindon hefty pattern; the Manor's is dainty by comparison). L.Elsey.

6803 BUCKLEBURY GRANGE
Built September 1936

Sheds and Works
17/10/36	Oxley
1/6/37	Shrewsbury
12/11/38	Swindon Works **I**
29/4/39	Swindon Works
29/4/39	Banbury
5/3/42	Swindon Works **I**
11/3/44	Swindon Works **HG**
15/6/46	Swindon Works **I**
12/7/48	Banbury Shops
29/1/49	Swindon Works **HI**
26/3/49	Swindon Works
27/1/51	Swindon Works **HI**
16/6/51	Stourbridge
6/9/52	Swindon Works **HC**
2/3/54	Swindon Works **HG**
15/11/55	Swindon Works **LC**
29/6/56	Swindon Works HI
7/8/58	Wolverhampton Works **HC**
16/7/60	Tyseley
11/5/60	Wolverhampton Works **HI**
1/1/62	Swindon Works **HC**
6/10/62	Oxley
25/10/63	Swindon Works **HG**

Tenders
From new	2150
1940	2107
1944	2329
1946	2118
1950	2372
1952	2822
1954	2162 2614
1956	2431 2247 [29/6/56]
1958	1894
1960	2141
1962	2256 [21/2/62]

NO OTHER DETAILS FOUND
Withdrawn 25/9/65

BUCKLEBURY GRANGE at Birmingham Snow Hill; the shed plate 84C is that of Banbury; 6803 had been there since 1939 and was transferred to Stourbridge in June 1951. If the plate was changed when it should have been then this is about 1950-51 and an indication that the dire external condition of Banbury Granges with which we became familiar in the 1960s had a long and proud tradition! transporttreasury

Post-Nationalisation Grange, 6803 BUCKLEBURY GRANGE near Wearde signal box west of Plymouth in April 1949. R.E. Vincent, transporttreasury

6804 BROCKINGTON GRANGE
Built September 1936

Mileages and Boilers
9/36		7209
22/8/38	80,445	7209
9/12/40	167,108	7209
11/12/42	234,686	C4479
26/2/45	299,491	C4479
7/6/47	380,630	C4931
9/8/49	449,484	C4435
12/10/51	527,312	C4026
27/7/54	607,508	C4909
3/1/57	702,505	C6204
20/11/59	810,134	C6205

Sheds and Works
19/9/36	St Philips Marsh
26/10/37	St. Philips Marsh Shops **R**
22/8/38	Swindon Works **I**
2/2/40	St. Philips Marsh Shops **R**
9/12/40	Swindon Works **I**
19/2/42	St. Philips Marsh **L**
18/8/42	St. Philips Marsh **R**
12/12/42	Swindon Works **HG**
12/1942	Westbury
15/9/43	Westbury Shops **R**
26/11/43	Severn Tunnel Jct. Shops **R**
26/2/45	Swindon Works **I**
10/9/45	Westbury Shops **R**
4/12/45	Reading Shops **R**
8/7/46	Westbury Shops **R**
4/10/46	Westbury Shops **R**
7/6/47	Swindon Works **I**
12/3/48	Bath Road Shops **R**
31/12/48	Bath Road Shops **R**
9/8/49	Swindon Works **HG**
2/12/50	St Philips Marsh
17/9/51	Swindon Works **HG**
28/5/53	Bath Road Shops **U**
24/12/53	Swindon Works **LC**
27/7/54	Swindon Works **HI**
3/1/57	Swindon Works **HG**
18/10/57	St. Philips Marsh **U**
2/3/59	Westbury Shops **U**
20/11/59	Swindon Works **HG**
14/2/61	Newton Abbot Works **U**
25/2/61	Laira
16/3/61	Taunton Shops **U**
19/4/61	Taunton Shops **U**
12/7/61	Penzance Shops **U**
9/11/61	Gloucester Shops **U**
11/8/62	Llanelly
20/12/62	Wolverhampton Works **LC**
30/11/63	St Philips Marsh
22/6/64	Barrow Road

Tenders
From new	2329
19/2/42	1766
11/12/42	2904
26/2/45	2873
7/6/47	1980
9/8/48	1934
12/10/51	2535
3/11/51	2250
24/12/53	2367
27/7/54	2741

Mileage at 28/12/63 904,632
Withdrawn 10/8/64

6804 BROCKINGTON GRANGE taking water at Bristol Temple Meads, 9 September 1956. The tender record ends at 1954 but it seems improbable that 6804 kept 4,000 gallon example 2741 for over a decade, through to withdrawal. E. Sawford, transporttreasury

At its then Home St Philips Marsh in the later 1950s; note modified, larger cover above steam pipe for the oil pipes to the cylinders and the smokebox-mounted regulator. J. Davenport, Initial Photographics.

Laira's BROCKINGTON GRANGE at St Blazey shed, 14 July 1961; dart-shaped cover this side too, as was (almost) universal with the loco in much better condition altogether. Taller chimney – it looks like – without capuchon, electrification flashes and high 4,000 gallon tender with second emblem, loose and missing washout plug covers on firebox shoulder – a common feature by now. R.C. Riley, transporttreasury

6805 BROUGHTON GRANGE

Built September 1936

Mileages and Boilers

Date	Mileage	Boiler
9/36		7210
5/1/39	93,378	7210
5/12/41	195,669	7210
17/8/44	277,146	C7243
7/8/46	352,420	C2829
23/7/48	422,940	C2906
8/9/50	510,499	C2981
4/3/53	606,313	C4027
26/7/55	689,032	C9284
24/1/58	774,484	C9284
22/3/61	878,233	C9284

Sheds and Works

21/9/36	Canton
12/11/38	Swindon Works I
10/1940	Old Oak Shops
27/10/41	Swindon Works I
7/1943	Swindon Works
4/7/44	Swindon Works HG
15/6/46	Swindon Works I
12/6/48	Swindon Works I
2/10/48	Pontypool Road
31/12/49	St Philips Marsh
12/8/50	Swindon Works HG
1/11/52	Swindon
24/1/53	Swindon Works HI
3/10/53	Swindon Works
1/2/55	Swindon Works LC
14/6/55	Swindon Works HG
28/12/57	Truro
24/1/58	Swindon Works HI
12/7/58	Laira
1/11/58	Truro
21/5/60	Penzance
18/6/60	Laira
8/10/60	Ebbw Jct.

Tenders

Date	Tender
From new	2367
5/1/39	2131
7/8/46	1895
9/10/47	2104
5/11/49	2265
8/9/50	2257
4/3/53	2253
24/9/53	2256
14/9/54	2760
1/2/55	2616
26/7/55	2623
11/1/57	2860

Final mileage 878,233
Withdrawn 22/3/61 Cut up 20/5/61

6805 BROUGHTON GRANGE heads 5017 THE GLOUCESTERSHIRE REGIMENT 28th, 61st out of Paddington past Ranelagh Bridge depot on 30 March 1957. The train is the 2.15pm Paddington-Cheltenham with an extra 'light' restaurant car at the front. 6805 would be returning to Swindon shed off the 7.5am Cheltenham-Paddington earlier. R.C. Riley, transporttreasury

6805 BROUGHTON GRANGE threads its way at Swindon in the summer of 1955, not long after a Heavy General there; it might well be on a running in turn. J.Robertson, transporttreasury

6806 BLACKWELL GRANGE

Built September 1936

Mileages and Boilers

Date	Mileage	Boiler
30/9/36		7211
20/7/39	91,189	7211
26/7/41	169,273	7211
9/1/44	254,622	C4971
19/3/46	332,964	C2840
2/6/48	412,905	C4061
11/1/51	525,529	R9290
29/5/53	611,671	R9290
10/11/55	699,507	C8279
5/11/57	788,063	C8211
22/8/60	866,169	C7220
8/2/63	934,355	C9289

Sheds and Works

17/10/36	Landore
27/8/37	Swindon Works **R**
11/5/38	Swindon Works **L**
30/7/39	Swindon Works **I**
26/7/41	Swindon Works **I**
10/9/43	Swindon Works **R**
9/1/44	Swindon Works **HG**
16/5/45	Landore Shops **R**
30/9/45	Bath Road Shops **R**
19/3/46	Swindon Works **I**
28/2/47	Landore Shops **L**
31/5/47	Carmarthen Shops **R**
29/1/48	Landore Shops **L**
	Tender work only
18/3/48	Old Oak Shops **L**
	Tender work only
2/6/48	Swindon Works **I**
9/7/48	Canton Shops **L**
30/10/48	Penzance
4/5/49	Laira Shops **U**
14/7/49	Newton Abbot Works **U**
28/10/49	Newton Abbot Works **U**
11/1/51	Swindon Works **HG**
14/8/51	Newton Abbot Works **U**
15/11/51	Penzance Shops **U**
1/8/52	Penzance Shops **U**
29/5/53	Swindon Works **HI**
19/8/53	Laira Shops **U**
9/10/54	Chester
16/10/54	Shrewsbury Shops **U**
9/1/55	Worcester Shops **U**
16/7/55	Hereford
16/7/55	Hereford Shops **U**
19/9/55	Croes Newydd Shops **U**
10/11/55	Swindon Works **HI**
31/12/55	Penzance
1/12/56	Oxley
28/8/57	Canton Shops **U**
8/11/57	Swindon Works **HG**
20/12/57	Wolverhampton Works **U**
6/11/58	Wolverhampton Works **LC**
14/8/59	Oxley Shops **U**
22/1/60	Oxley Shops **U**
4/6/60	Southall Shops **U**
22/8/60	Swindon Works **HG**
10/3/61	Oxley Shops **U**
15/7/61	Worcester
28/7/61	Ebbw Jct. Shops **U**
6/9/61	Exeter Shops **U**
9/3/62	Worcester Shops **U**
8/2/63	Swindon Works **HI**
9/7/64	Worcester shops **U**

Tenders

Date	Tender
From new	1880
20/7/39	2125
26/7/41	2077
9/1/44	2204
19/3/46	1877
2/6/48	1952
8/10/49	2242
29/5/53	2257
10/11/55	2433
22/8/60	2752
8/2/63	2928

Mileage at 28/12/63 958,246
Withdrawn 23/10/64

In post-overhaul condition on a spur off that turntable at Swindon, probably after its Heavy General in 1960.

BLACKWELL GRANGE waiting for the signals in Birmingham Snow Hill with a down freight, 30 April 1957; 4,000 gallon tender. Michael Mensing.

6807 BIRCHWOOD GRANGE

Built September 1936

Mileages and Boilers

Date	Mileage	Boiler
9/36		7212
5/10/38	82,431	7212
24/7/40	147,517	7212
9/4/43	238,246	9220
26/4/45	312,286	4443
22/6/48	410,071	7234
10/1/50	471,034	4994
16/11/51	544,528	4472
23/2/54	631,141	4423
21/3/56	701,524	2825
6/6/58	792,286	2825
27/9/60	864,008	6246

Sheds and Works

28/9/36	Worcester
17/1/38	Worcester Shops **R**
5/10/38	Swindon Works **I**
24/7/40	Swindon Works **I**
9/4/43	Swindon Works **HG**
4/1/45	Worcester Shops **R**
26/4/45	Swindon Works **I**
16/5/46	Worcester Shops **R**
20/12/46	Canton Tender change only
19/4/47	Worcester Shops **L**
22/6/48	Swindon Works **I**
10/1/50	Swindon Works **HG**
14/6/51	Worcester Shops **U**
16/11/51	Swindon Works **HI**
23/2/54	Swindon Works **HG**
8/6/55	Worcester Shops **U**
21/3/56	Swindon Factory **HG**
6/6/58	Wolverhampton Works **HI**
26/6/59	Gloucester Shops **U**
3/5/60	Gloucester Barnwood Shops **U**
22/9/60	Swindon Factory **HG**
2/12/61	Gloucester Barnwood Shops **U**
9/2/62	Ebbw Jct. Shops **U**
28/2/62	Ebbw Jct. Shops **U**
12/4/62	Worcester Factory **U**
20/2/63	Worcester Shops **U**

Tenders

Date	Tender
From new	1988
9/4/43	2922
26/4/45	2219
2/11/46	2257
23/6/48	1877
30/6/49	2539
10/1/50	2084
16/11/51	2448
2/10/52	1560
12/11/53	2253
29/6/54	2367
18/1/58	2579
27/9/60	2446

Final mileage 954,048
Withdrawn 28/12/63 Sold to A King Norwich 28/2/64

A Worcester engine all its life, 6807 was frequently to be found in London. Here it is in 'overall grey' livery, at Old Oak Common on 18 June 1960; capuchon, washout plug covers absent. BIRCHWOOD GRANGE is soon to go to Swindon for a major overhaul – see opposite.

In unlined black with tall capuchon chimney at Worcester shed, 14 June 1953, 6807 BIRCHWOOD GRANGE is still in fairly good external nick at Worcester shed. This picture is fortuitous for it shows Dean tender No.1560 (it was with 6807 for just a year) rebuilt with body having a Collett fender; G and W either side of the later crest, the twin shields of Bristol and London. Norman Preedy Archive.

In sparkling condition after overhaul at Swindon. Lined green with 4,000 gallon tender; yet another form of covering boiler/smokebox. This is the Heavy General of 1960 (note electrification flashes) when 6807 received a brand new boiler and improved draughting with caphuchon-less chimney. J. Davenport, Initial Photographics.

6808 BEENHAM GRANGE
Built September 1936

Sheds and Works
3/10/36	Penzance
5/2/38	Newton Abbot Works
4/2/39	Swindon Works I
1/1940	Newton Abbot Works
3/1940	Exeter
6/1940	Swindon Works
17/7/41	Swindon Works I
1/42	Penzance
2/4/44	Swindon Works G
18/5/44	Newton Abbot
1/44	Penzance
13/10/47	Swindon Works I
9/8/49	Swindon Works HG
10/9/51	Swindon Works HI
6/11/53	Swindon Works HG
19/4/56	Wolverhampton Works HI
11/1/58	Swindon Works HG
22/9/59	In store
15/8/61	Swindon Works HI
7/9/62-1963	Cardiff, East Dock
4/3/63	Llanelly
9/9/63-1964	Oxley

Tenders
From new	1889
1940	1780
1942	2005
1944	1904
1946	1926
1948	2039
1950	2237
1952	2657
1954	2908
1958	1719 2262 [6/2/58]
1962	2834

NO FURTHER DETAIL

Withdrawn 8/64

Left. 6808 BEENHAM GRANGE, a West Country engine for the great part of its life, on typical summer Saturday work for a Grange, piloting an express out of Plymouth North Road, full of returning holidaymakers. RailOnline.

Below. In fine condition, in unlined black, at Laira shed, 5 August 1954. J. Robertson, transporttreasury

6809 BURGHCLERE GRANGE

Built September 1936

Mileages and Boilers

Date	Mileage	Boiler
9/36		7214
7/7/38	85,616	7214
3/4/40	159,935	7214
26/5/42	225,903	C2945
9/6/45	326,235	C4029
21/10/47	409,166	C2976
23/12/49	485,835	C2866
16/8/51	567,277	C4900
22/10/53	664,078	C4900
28/11/55	759,990	C9286
27/11/57	849,095	C9286
11/7/60	943,538	C4980

Sheds and Works

4/10/36	Old Oak Common
7/7//38	Swindon Works I
3/4/40	Swindon Works I
10/7/41	Swindon Works L
26/5/42	Swindon Works HG
17/942	Old Oak Shops R
30/7/43	Old Oak Shops R
17/3/44	Swindon Works L
7/7/44	Old Oak Shed R
28/12/44	Old Oak Shops R
9/6/45	Swindon Shed I
27/11/45	Old Oak Shops R
14/6/46	Southall
26/6/47	Southall Shops R
21/10/47	Swindon Works I
5/8/48	Old Oak Shops R
3/8/49	Southall Shops U
1/11/49	Old Oak Shops U
23/12/49	Swindon Works HG
23/12/49	Penzance
16/8/51	Swindon Works HG
22/10/53	Swindon Works HI
20/6/55	Penzance Shops U
28/11/55	Swindon Works HG
15/4/56	Penzance Shops U
9/6/56	Penzance Shops U
12/9/57	Newton Abbot Works HI
28/12/57	Pontypool Road
22/5/58	St Philip's Marsh
22/1/60	Oxley Shops U
11/7/60	Swindon Works HG
30/5/61	Taunton Shops U
15/3/62	Llanelly Shops U
13/4/62	St. Philips Marsh Shops U
6/10/62	Southall
3/12/62	Oxley Shops U
15/5/63	Southall Shops U

Tenders

Date	Tender
From new	1949
10/7/41	2125
26/5/42	2890
17/9/42	2340
9/6/45	2039
21/10/47	1898
22/10/53	2535
4/8/54	2431
28/11/55	2562
2/7/57	1898
27/11/57	2581
11/7/60	2245

Final mileage 1,024,508
Withdrawn 1/7/63 Cut up 7/9/63

6809 BURGHCLERE GRANGE (it had acquired lined black in December 1949) with down broccoli empties (not cattle!) at Lipson Vale, 21 February 1951. It had been at Southall after the War but by now was a Penzance engine, and thus hardly/never to seen near London. Low sided 3,500 gallon tender. Mention was made in the introductory section *New Locos For Old* of BAMPTON GRANGE getting to Portsmouth, somewhat illegally it turns out, for clearances for the new locos had not been established. In the autumn of 1938, two years later, 6809 BURGHCLERE GRANGE was in turn engaged in a series of tests of platform and bridge clearances to Eastleigh and Portsmouth and other points south including Reading to Ascot. The engine was sent from Reading, and a Southern 3rd class brake composite coach provided at Basingstoke for the travelling inspectors. 6809 returned to Eastleigh shed every night from 25 October 1938 to 30 October 1938 – a temporary allocation if you like! Granges and Manors were cleared to work over the Southern between Reading and Ascot in early 1939 – this was important not least because of the lucrative Ascot race traffic, which had previously had to be given over to 43XX 2-6-0s. This, as in so many other ways, is how the new 4-6-0s ousted the old moguls. Alan Lathey, transporttreasury

BURGHCLERE GRANGE at St Philips Marsh shed, about 1959; now in rather battle-worn lined green. It had got the 4,000 gallon tender at the end of 1957. Much larger cover on smokebox. The light angle shows how the ejector pipe bent down behind the reversing shaft before entering the cab. J. Davenport, Initial Photographics.

6809 at Bristol Temple Meads. A boiler change has seen a reversion to the early dart-shaped cover; electrification flashes and the 'intermediate' 3,500 gallon tender, from July 1960. 'Economy size' train reporting number 2B96 above buffer beam denotes the 9.40am Temple Meads to Weston Super Mare.

6809 with coal empties but looking good, climbing Filton bank past Horfield on the edge of Bristol with a northbound goods, September 1961. Norman Preedy Archive.

Back at Southall, still with 'intermediate' tender, 4 November 1962. Peter Groom.
J. Davenport, Initial Photographics.

6810 BLAKEMERE GRANGE

Built November 1936

Mileages and boilers

Date	Mileage	Boiler
11/36		7215
25/2/39	90,349	7215
16/5/42	204,384	7215
27/10/44	294,022	C7210
26/6/47	387,543	C2954
4/1/50	475,669	C8236
27/5/52	558,420	C2817
10/1/55	644,843	C7230
15/5/57	725,444	C7230
3/11/59	805,520	C2912
2/11/62	903,781	C7224

Sheds and Works

12/12/36	Canton
25/2/39	Swindon Works **I**
10/6/41	Swindon Works **L**
16/5/42	Swindon Works **I**
19/12/42	Canton Shops **L**
13/3/43	Swindon Works **R**
13/9/44	Swindon Works **HG**
20/9/43	Canton Shops **L**
27/10/44	Swindon Works **HG**
16/3/45	Canton Shops **L**
2/8/46	Canton Shops **R**
14/12/46	Landore Shops **R**
26/6/47	Canton Shops **I**
6/10//47	Swindon Works **I**
2/5/48	Severn Tunnel Jct. Shops **L**
12/6/48	Pontypool Road
2/10/48	Llanelly
11/10/49	Oxford Shops **U**
4/1/50	Swindon Works **HG**
15/1/51	Llanelly Shops **U**
27/5/52	Swindon Works **HG**
21/9/53	Llanelly Shops **U**
10/1/55	Swindon Works **HG**
24/4/56	Duffryn Road Shops **U**
15/5/57	Swindon Works **HI**
20/7/57	Oxford Shops **U**
30/8/58	Llanelly Shops **U**
3/11/59	Swindon Works **HG**
7/10/61	Pontypool Road
12/2/62	Pontypool Road Shops **U**
2/11/62	Swindon Works **HI**
21/11/62	Ebbw Jct. Shops **U**
19/6/63	Swindon Works **U**
29/6/63	Neath
26/6/64	Llanelly

Tenders

Date	Tender
From new	1912
16/5/42	2289
20/9/43	2029
27/10/44	1986
16/3/45	2214
29/1/49	1759
27/5/52	2248
10/1/55	2250
3/11/59	2791
2/11/62	2778

Mileage at 28/12/63 932,404
Withdrawn 23/10/64

6810 BLAKEMERE GRANGE at Old Oak Common shed, 20 May 1956; 'intermediate' tender. R.C. Riley, transporttreasury

CHESFORD GRANGE after an Intermediate at Swindon in October 1962. L.W. Rowe, ColourRail.

CHESFORD GRANGE on one of the roads that led out of the back of the roundhouses at Tyseley, 6 August 1963. This was space set aside for enlarging the roundhouses, work which was never carried out. The public road was some hundred yards away and it provided the unusual spectacle, especially from the top of a bus, of a loco standing alone, apparently unattended, in what was a field. J.L. Stevenson, courtesy Hamish Stevenson.

6813 EASTBURY GRANGE
Built December 1936

Mileages and Boilers

Date	Mileage	Boiler
12/36		7218
1/4/39	90,773	7218
18/8/41	187,846	7218
2/7/43	236,476	C7269
4/5/46	311,510	C2834
4/3/49	386,485	C9222
20/9/51	466,978	C4453
12/3/54	562,828	C2814
20/6/56	654,711	C8276
11/7/58	737,595	C4949
16/2/61	831,097	C4487

Sheds and Works

12/12/36	Exeter
17/10/38	Newton Abbot Works **L**
1/4/39	Swindon Works **I**
3/1940	Penzance
28/5/40	Penzance Shops **R**
22/10/40	Newton Abbot Shops **L**
18/8/41	Swindon Works **I**
9/1941	Newton Abbot
28/8/42	Newton Abbot Works **R**
2/7/43	Swindon Works **HG**
10/8/43	Goodwick **R**
5/6/45	Newton Abbot Shed **R**
14/5/46	Swindon Works **I**
20/9/46	Newton Abbot Works **R**
4/2/48	Newton Abbot Works **R**
4/3/49	Swindon Works **HG**
2/12/50	Newton Abbot Works **LC**
20/9/51	Swindon Works **HI**
5/11/57	Newton Abbot Works **LC**
11/758	Swindon Works **HG**
16/5/60	Newton Abbot Shed **U**
21/5/60	Exeter
8/10/60	Ebbw Jct.
16/2/61	Swindon Works **HG**
19/6/62	Ebbw Jct. Shops **U**
19/7/62	Ebbw Jct. Shops **U**
3/4/63	Caerphilly Works **LC**
9/12/63	Swindon Works **HI**
10/4/64	Swindon Works **LC**
22/6/64	Worcester

Tenders

Date	Tender
From new	1921
1/4/39	1983
18/8/41	2350
2/7/43	2227
4/3/49	2118
12/3/54	2608
20/6/56	2431
11/7/58	2248
16/2/61	2251
9/12/63	2651

Mileage at 28/12/63 900,085
Withdrawn 10/9/65

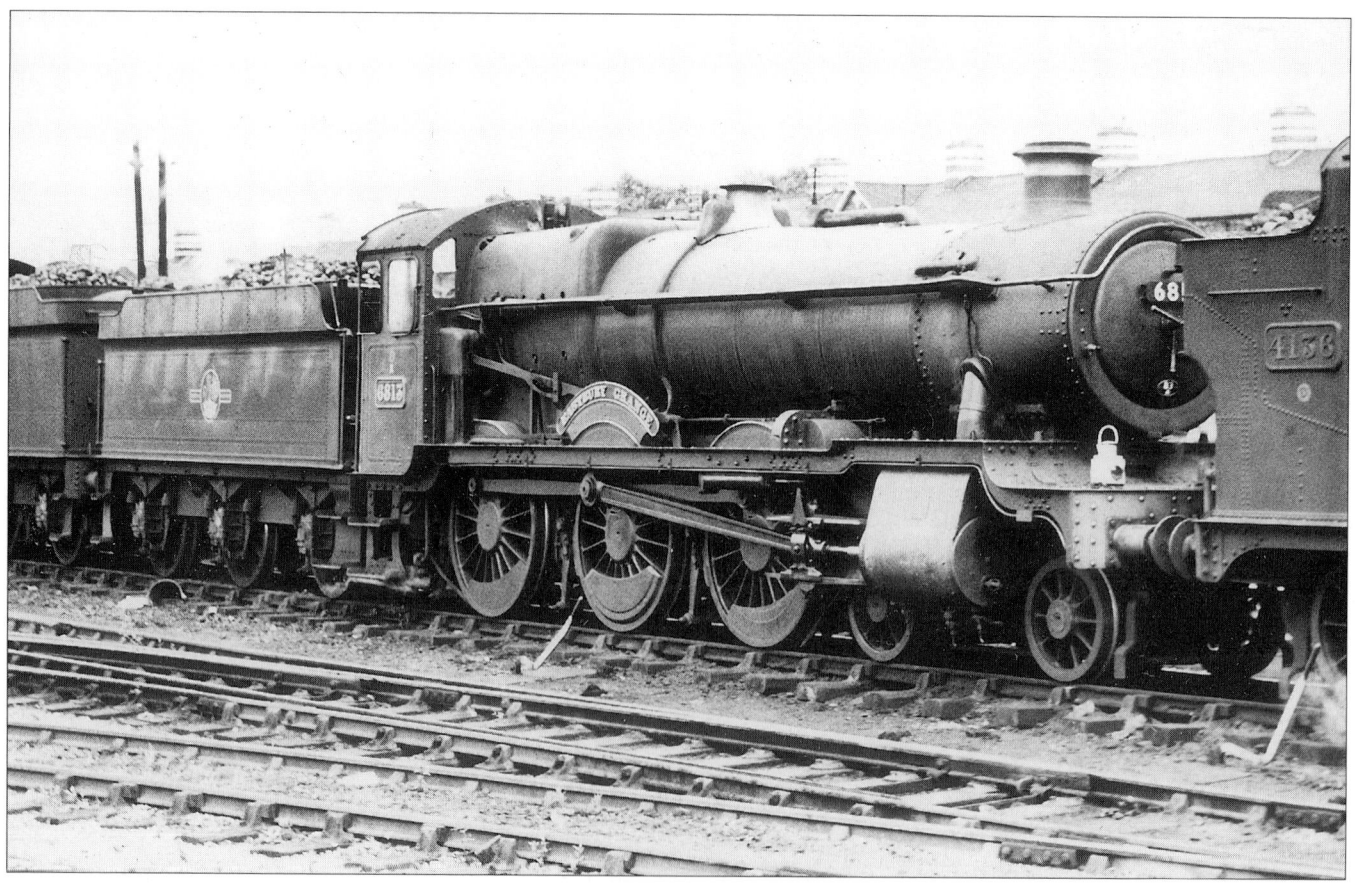

6813 at Newton Abbot shed about 1959, now in lined green with 'intermediate' 3,500 gallon tender. Shows nicely the drop down compared to the 4,000 gallon to the rear. J. Davenport, Initial Photographics.

6813 EASTBURY GRANGE at Exeter St David's, 7 August 1954 with a train for the North of England headed by an LMS coach; 4,000 gallon tender. J. Robertson, transporttreasury

6814 ENBORNE GRANGE
Built December 1936

Mileages and Boilers

Date	Mileage	Boiler
12/36		7219
24/4/39	93,136	7219
8/4/42	198,766	7219
11/1/44	242,968	C4993
12/9/45	284,912	C4435
26/7/49	376,781	C4472
29/10/51	449,329	C2829
7/4/54	541,709	C2994
3/8/56	634,993	C2988
21/8/58	719,197	C2869
26/1/61	803,483	C9290

Sheds and Works

12/12/36	Exeter
26/4/39	Swindon Works I
3/1941	Newton Abbot
8/4/42	Swindon Works I
11/1/44	Swindon Works L
12/9/45	Swindon Works HG
5/12/46	Newton Abbot Shed R
18/6/47	Newton Abbot Works
29/8/47	Newton Abbot Shed R
22/10/47	Newton Abbot Works L
6/2/48	Newton Abbot Works L
	Tender Work only
26/7/49	Swindon Works HG
14/11/50	Newton Abbot Works LC
14/8/51	Newton Abbot Shed U
30/8/51	Laira Shops U
29/10/51	Swindon Works HI
12/12/51	Newton Abbot Works U
20/5/53	Newton Abbot Shed U
2/12/53	Laira Shops U
11/1/54	Newton Abbot Shed U
7/4/54	Swindon Works HG
16/6/55	Newton Abbot Shed U
3/8/56	Swindon Works HI
22/2/58	St. Blazey
21/8/58	Swindon Works HG
20/5/60	Newton Abbot Works U
3/9/60	Taunton Shops U
5/11/60	Exeter
26/1/61	Swindon Works HI
25/2/61	Penzance
6/6/62	St. Philips Marsh
14/8/62	St. Philips Marsh Shops U
31/12/62	St. Philips Marsh Shops
1/4/63	St. Philips Marsh Shops U
2/8/63	Worcester shops U

Tenders

Date	Tender
From new	2157
26/4/39	2319
8/4/42	2179
14/1/44	1983
12/9/45	2906
26/7/49	1876
29/10/51	2608
7/4/54	2118
3/8/56	2626
21/8/58	2116
26/1/61	2243

Mileage as at 16/12/63 874,549
Withdrawn 16/12/63 Cut up 25/1/64

Its tender and chimney a contrast to that of 6875 HINDFORD GRANGE behind, 6814 ENBORNE GRANGE heads a train of milk tankers at Aller Junction, August 1955. The tall chimney with capuchon, as shown on pages 24, 29, 31 and others and on 6814 here, derives from Saint or early Hall Standard No.1 boilers. The height difference between this chimney and the usual shorter one (on 6875, say) is ably illustrated here. There was another style of tall chimney, with no capuchon; this originated in a programme of improved draughting applied to all post-Group Swindon 4-6-0 classes in the later 1950s. It became very common on Granges as more and more Swindon No.1 boilers were modified. J. Robertson, transporttreasury

ENBORNE GRANGE at Reading, 1958, now in the lined green. Michael Boakes Collection.

Now at Old Oak Common on 22 August 1963, 6814 has acquired a 3,500 gallon 'intermediate' tender; the lined green is still there, just, under the grime. Peter Groom.

6815 FRILFORD GRANGE
Built December 1936

Mileages and Boilers
12/36		2914
12/8/39	90,132	2914
19/3/42	171,834	2914
29/3/45	276,295	C2976
7/10/47	367,719	C8284
16/8/50	475,034	C2833
28/1/53	582,437	C9220
27/5/55	678,673	C4922
15/8/57	767,498	C6215
6/11/59	863,539	C6222
26/4/63	946,196	C2981

Sheds and Works
12/12/36	Exeter
9/1/37	Oxley
13/3/37	Swindon Works **L**
29/5/37	Chester
29/439	Banbury
12/8/39	Wolverhampton Works **I**
16/9/39	Ebbw Jct.
11/6/40	Didcot Shops **L**
13/5/41	Shrewsbury Shops **R**
19/3/42	Swindon Works **I**
29/3/45	Swindon Works **HG**
25/147	Severn Tunnel Junction
4/6/47	Severn Tunnel Jct. Shops **R**
7/10/47	Swindon Works **I**
10/7/48	Taunton
28/2/49	Taunton Shops **U**
8/7/49	Banbury Shops **U**
19/8/49	Newton Abbot Works **LC**
16/8/50	Swindon Works **HG**
28/1/53	Swindon Works **HG**
10/12/53	Newton Abbot Works **LC**
2/4/54	Taunton Shops **U**
27/5/55	Swindon Works **HG**
28/3/57	Newton Abbot Works **U**
15/8/57	Swindon Works **HG**
6/11/59	Swindon Works **HG**
24/2/61	Taunton Shops **U**
17/6/61	Laira
19/7/61	Penzance Shops **U**
14/9/61	Taunton Shops **U**
11/8/62	Llanelly
22/2/63	Worcester Shops **U**
26/4/63	Swindon Works **HI**
1/10/63	Swindon Works **HI cont**
20/8/64	Llanelly Shops **U**
7/11/64	Cardiff East Dock
7/8/65	Severn Tunnel Jct.

Tenders
From new	1744
19/3/42	2873
29/3/45	2901
16/8/50	1777
28/1/53	2699
17/5/55	2042
15/8/57	2395
6/11/59	2266
26/4/63	2244

Mileage at 28/12/63 955,954
Withdrawn 18/11/65

Taunton's 6815 FRILFORD GRANGE with a down train at Burngullow, 21 June 1955. Alan Lathey, transporttreasury

6815 in much reduced circumstances, with 'intermediate' 3,500 gallon tender at Southall shed on 19 September 1965, after working up from its last shed, Severn Tunnel Junction. It is in fact in a better-looking state than many by this time, though the nameplate (including its supporting struts) has gone. It might have been on some tour in recent months, for it had been noted at Gloucester Horton Road a couple of months before 'in an exceptionally fine condition'. RailOnline.

6815 with 9F 92128 on 13 March 1965; a familiar enough scene at Banbury shed by then. J.L. Stevenson, courtesy Hamish Stevenson.

6816 FRANKTON GRANGE
Built December 1936

Mileages and Boilers
From new		2922
8/7/39	88,317	2922
10/1/43	192,317	C2922
29/8/44	239,336	C2982
14/6/46	290,463	C4464
5/5/49	385,984	C8285
7/6/51	466,918	C2889
29/12/53	553,550	C7255
22/6/56	672,330	C7255
6/1/59	776,458	C9201
26/9/61	877,006	C8276
3/3/64	932,597	C8289

Sheds and Works
6/2/37	Oxley
29/5/37	Chester
8/7/39	Stafford Road Shops **I**
22/7/39	Oxley
19/8/39	Banbury
14/10/39	Stafford Road Shops **R**
22/5/41	Banbury Shops **R**
17/9/41	Gloucester Shops **R**
8/1/42	Old Oak Shops **R**
14/8/42	Tyseley Shops **R**
10/1/43	Swindon Works **I**
8/2/43	Newton Abbot Works **R**
2/6/43	Laira Shops **R**
29/8/44	Swindon Works **L**
24/11/44	Westbury Shops **R**
11/7/45	Banbury Shops **R**
30/4/46	Bath Road Shops **R**
14/6/46	Swindon Works **I**
22/12/47	Stourbridge Shops **R**
16/3/48	Banbury Shops **R**
1/9/48	Banbury Shops **R**
28/10/48	Banbury Shops **R**
2/2/49	Banbury Shops **U**
5/5/49	Swindon Works **HG**
30/6/50	Banbury Shops **U**
13/9/50	Banbury Shops **U**
7/6/51	Swindon Works **HG**
5/11/52	Exeter Shops **U**
21/2/53	Landore
16/5/53	Laira
29/12/53	Swindon Works **HG**
22/7/55	Laira Shops **U**
22/6/56	Newton Abbot Works **HI**
25/2/57	Laira Shops **U**
13/8/57	Laira Shops **U**
2/1/58	Laira Shops **U**
22/258	Penzance
6/1/59	Swindon Works **HG**
2/2/59	Penzance (store)
21/5/60	Laira
8/10/60	St. Philips Marsh
6/4/61	St. Philips Marsh Shops **U**
26/9/61	Swindon Works **HI**
15/11/62	Wolverhampton Works **LC**
2/1/63	St. Philips Marsh Shops **U**
20/9/63	Westbury Shops **U**
3/3/64	Swindon Works **HC**
22/6/64	Barrow Road
10/7/65	Worcester

Tenders
From new	2164
24/11/44	1922
14/6/46	2917
5/5//49	2121
17/6/51	2038
29/12/53	2250
11/9/54	2535
6/12/54	2438
26/1/57	2561
8/12/58	1684
26/9/61	2257
3/3/64	2881

Mileage at 28/12/63 932,597
Withdrawn 21/7/65

6816 FRANKTON GRANGE at Bristol Temple Meads, 1958; tall chimney, 'intermediate' 3,500 gallon tender. Michael Boakes Collection.

6816 on 3 June 1962, outside the old shed at Oxford, barely altered since it was built. To the left is the ironically named 'Top Shop', which was not much more than a covered hoist. Note how 6816's hand rail curves to accommodate the ejector pipe. RailOnline.

Engines still flickered into life with overhauls and repaints even as late as 1964, when some were being scrapped. This is 6816 splendidly turned out at Swindon in spring 1964. It had gone in from St Philips Marsh (82B) but actually went 'home' to 82E Barrow Road, the ex-LMR shed, 'The Marsh' having closed in the meantime!

6817 GWENDDWR GRANGE
Built December 1936

Mileages and Boilers

From new		2930
30/3/39	93,881	2930
23/10/41	191,904	2930
29/4/44	275,598	C7247
16/5/46	359,474	C7207
26/10/48	452,596	C4443
23/4/51	555,401	C9206
18/3/53	641,034	C4421
28/10/55	750,647	C4421
1/10/57	812,907	C8225
3/2/60	894,342	C7225
1/10/62	967,456	C7208

Sheds and Works

12/12/36	Canton
30/3/39	Swindon Works I
29/10/40	Canton Shops R
23/10/41	Swindon Works I
13/10/42	Canton Shops R
3/9/43	Canton Shops L
13/10/43	Canton Shops R
29/4/44	Swindon Works G
2/6/45	Canton Shops R
24/8/45	Old Oak Shops R
16/5/46	Swindon Works I
3/6/47	Severn Tunnel Jct Shops R
22/6/47	Canton R
22/8/47	Canton R
3/9/47	Newton Abbot Works L
17/10/47	Canton Shops R
7/4/48	Canton Shops L
	Tender work only
12/6/48	Taunton
26/10/48	Swindon Works I
1/3/49	Taunton Shops U
23/4/49	Penzance
6/4/50	Newton Abbot Works U
23/1/51	Penzance Shops U
23/4/51	Swindon Works HG
3/10/52	Penzance Shops U
18/3//53	Swindon Works HG
9/10/54	Chester
24/10/55	Swindon Works HI
26/2/56	Chester Shops U
27/8/56	Stourbridge Shops U
27/2/57	Chester Shops U
17/7/57	Chester shops U
23/8/57	Old Oak Shops U
1/10/57	Swindon Works HG

Officially LMR loco with transfer of Chester 84K as 6E 23/2/58

14/6/58	Croes Newydd

Returned to WR book stock 15/6/58

12/7/58	Oxley
22/10/58	Gloucester Shops U
21/12/58	Wolverhampton Works LC
11/8/59	Oxley Shops U
22/9/59	Taunton Shops U
3/2/60	Swindon Works HG
19/9/60	Reading Shops U
2/12/60	Tyseley Shops U
15/7/61	Worcester
29/8/61	Worcester shops U
1/10/62	Swindon Works HI
13/3/64	Worcester Shops U

Tenders

From new	2131
15/10/38	2241
30/3/39	2367
29/4/44	1671
16/5/46	2005
26/10/48	2077
23/4/50	1985
23/4/51	2219
18/3/53	2642
57/10/55	2582
1/10/57	2577
3/2/60	2716
1/10/62	2249

Mileage to 28/12/63 1,000,984
Withdrawn 22/5/65

GWENDDWR GRANGE at Tyseley shed late on; 'intermediate' tender. Michael Boakes Collection.

6817 at Swindon shed, obviously after overhaul, in lined green, 7 February 1960; 4,000 gallon tender.

Dog days at Worcester, 12 October 1964. J.L. Stevenson, courtesy Hamish Stevenson.

6818 HARDWICK GRANGE
Built December 1936

Mileages and Boilers

Date	Mileage	Boiler
From new		2939
1/9/39	90,806	2939
7/8/42	193,839	2939
2/3/45	272,299	C8202
1/4/47	331,780	C2967
8/9/48	382,893	C7235
21/11/49	432,254	C8291
1/1/52	513,031	C4460
7/9/54	610,503	C8223
21/1/57	691,357	C4426
1/4/59	773,673	C2994
12/1/62	866,383	C2994

Sheds and Works

12/12/36	Ebbw Jct.
22/7/37	Ebbw Jct. Shops **R**
23/11/37	Ebbw Jct. Shops **R**
1/9/39	Swindon Works **I**
14/10/39	Pontypool Road
7/12/40	Pontypool Road Shops **R**
7/8/42	Swindon Works **I**
21/9/42	Tyseley Shops **R**
8/12/42	Ebbw Jct. Shops **R**
21/1/43	Hereford Shops **R**
12/8/44	Westbury Shops **R**
2/3/45	Swindon Works **HG**
31/5/46	Pontypool Road **R**
31/7/46	Ebbw Jct. Shops **L**
25/1/47	Neath
3/3/47	Swindon Works **I***
1/4/47	Swindon Works **I***
19/4/47	Carmarthen
29/4/48	Carmarthen Shops **R**
8/9/48	Swindon Works **L**
21/11/49	Swindon Works **HG**
13/10/50	Carmarthen Shops **U**
1/12/50	Carmarthen Shops **U**
1/1/52	Swindon Works **HG**
1/11/52	Llanelly
7/9/54	Swindon Works **HI**
21/1/57	Swindon Works **HG**
1/4/59	Swindon Works **HI**
26/7/60	Southall Shops **U**
20/8/60	Didcot Shops **U**
12/1/62	Swindon Works **HG**
24/2/64	Ebbw Jct.

*First if not both of these Intermediates the result of a single line collision with 9023 18/2/47; 6818 noted as still a Pontypool Road engine

Tenders

Date	Tender
From new	1908
2/3/45	1902
1/2/48	2334
1/7/48	1998
29/4/48	2029
26/3/49	2179
21/11/49	1989
26/2/50	2143
22/4/50	2253
1/1/52	2818
7/9/54	2668
11/1/57	2689
1/4/59	2247
12/1/62	2260

Mileage as at 28/12/63 926,686
Withdrawn 8/4/64 Sold to Birds Risca 3/6/64

HARDWICK GRANGE at Worcester Shrub Hill, 12 November 1963, with a southbound Class E goods. As was horribly typical as the 1960s moved on to the dismal finale, the Grange is absolutely filthy; while 'Great Western' cleaning was never the wonder some might have imagined the difference was quite marked to this youthful observer just in the years 1960-1964, when an overwhelming impression of green and brass gave way to grey and black. Colour Rail.

6818 HARDWICK GRANGE at Llanelly shed on 10 August 1957; lined green with 'intermediate' tender, small emblem. 6818 was only ever based at Welsh sheds. Dart-shaped cover above the steampipe, where the lubricating piping briefly emerged. J. Davenport, Initial Photographics.

6819 HIGHNAM GRANGE
Built December 1936

Mileages and Boilers

Date	Mileage	Boiler
From new		2946
12/5/39	99,840	2946
13/10/42	198,520	2946
23/5/44	242,676	C4925
11/7/45	281,344	C4925
17/2/47	341,928	C7224
14/9/49	421,171	C2947
25/2/52	497,561	C8270
20/1/55	589,551	C8270
8/10/57	675,767	C6213
30/6/60	769,087	C6213
13/3/63	804,512	C4991

Sheds and Works

12/12/36	Pontypool Road
12/5/39	Swindon Works I
27/5/39	Chester
12/5/39	Swindon Works I
1/8/40	Chester Shops R
22/8/41	Birkenhead Shops R
13/1042	Swindon Works I
14/10/42	Oxley
22/5/44	Swindon Works L
3/1/45	Oxley Shops R
11/7/45	Swindon Works I
8/9/45	Birkenhead
27/12/45	Swindon Works I
24/7/46	Swindon Works R
17/2/47	Swindon Works HG
23/9/48	Oxley Shops L
3/3/49	Swindon Works
14/9/49	Swindon Works HG
15/7/50	Banbury
6/11/51	Banbury Shops U
25/2/52	Swindon Works HG
11/7/53	Swindon
31/10/53	Ebbw Jct.
28/11/53	Pontypool Road
15/10/54	Pontypool Road Shops U
10/1/55	Caerphilly Works HI
2/7/56	Slough Shops U
2/10/57	Swindon Works HG
30/6/60	Wolverhampton Works HI
9/8/60	Banbury Shops U
7/9/60	Stourbridge Shops U
26/4/61	Pontypool Road Shops U
17/6/61	Ebbw Jct.
10/8/61	Ebbw Jct. Shops U
9/9/61	Pontypool Road
31/10/61	Pontypool Road Shops U
23/7/62	Caerphilly Works LC
18/1/63	Pontypool Road Shops U
13/3/63	Swindon Works HI
6/11/63	Swindon Works HI cont
22/6/64	Worcester

Tenders

Date	Tender
From new	2075
12/5/39	1750
23/5/44	2899
11/7/45	2888
17/2/47	1906
23/9/48	2325
25/2/52	2255
30/1/55	2616
3/10/57	2645
13/3/63	2393

Mileage as at 28/12/63 820,491
Withdrawn 18/11/65

Looking dainty and Manor-like before the War, 6819 HIGHNAM GRANGE has the tall chimney with capuchon and first tender style with the 'shirt button' roundel. The livery would be plain green. transporttreasury

HIGHNAM GRANGE was one of the two Granges to get the lined black livery, in January 1955, at Caerphilly works where instructions perhaps had not been received, or were discounted. This is 6819 when it was a Pontypool Road engine with a train for Birmingham near Stratford upon Avon on 16 August 1958. It had gone into Swindon for a Heavy General late the previous year where the lined black was 'corrected' to lined green and the second tender emblem applied. W. Wilson, transporttreasury

And here it is in that lined black, at Shrewsbury shed.

6820 KINGSTONE GRANGE

Built January 1937

Mileages and Boilers

From new		7220
7/9/39	93,747	7220
20/11/42	198,896	7220
22/2/45	271,776	C8274
26/7/47	349,194	C4406
13/6/50	432,102	C8250
30/12/52	528,991	C2939
9/8/55	628,873	C9289
23/12/57	726,964	C9208
29/4/60	816,274	C2803
31/10/63	898,860	C7263

Sheds and Works

6/3/37	Ebbw Jct.
1/4/38	Ebbw Jct. Shops **R**
7/9/39	Wolverhampton Works **I**
14/10/39	Canton
2/1940	Pontypool Road
2/3/40	Carmarthen Shops **R**
21/11/40	Swindon Works **L**
1/12/41	Hereford Shops **R**
14/8/42	Ebbw Jct. Shops **R**
20/11/42	Swindon Works **I**
12/1/44	Worcester Shops **R**
16/3/44	Pontypool Road Shops **R**
22/2/45	Swindon Works **HG**
26/6/45	Carmarthen Shops **R**
29/12/45	Carmarthen Shops **R**
18/9/46	Reading Shops **L**
14/11/46	Old Oak Shops **L**
9/3/47	Pontypool Road **R**
26/7/47	Swindon Works **I**
16/2/48	Ebbw Jct. Shops **R**
27/11/48	Ebbw Jct.
16/9/49	Swindon Shed **U**
16/1/50	Newton Abbot Works **U**
13/6/50	Swindon Works **HG**
2/9/52	Swindon Works **U**
30/12/52	Swindon Works **HI**
2/9/53	Ebbw Jct. Shops **U**
23/4/54	Caerphilly Works **LC**
9/8/55	Swindon Works **HG**
16/6/56	Exeter
12/8/57	Exeter Shops **U**
5/10/57	Exeter Shops **U**
5/10/57	Worcester
23/12/57	Swindon Works **HI**
29/4/60	Swindon Works **HG**
28/2/61	Worcester Shops **U**
22/4/61	Pontypool Road
15/6/61	Pontypool Road Shops **U**
17/6/61	Ebbw Jct.
6/7/61	Ebbw Jct. Shops **U**
8/3/62	Swindon Works **HC**
By 3/63?	Pontypool Road
10/4/63	Severn Tunnel Jct. Shops **U**
2/7/63	Cathays **U**
31/10/63	Swindon Works **HI**
22/6/64	Cardiff East Dock

Tenders

From new	2348
20/11/42	2902
22/2/45	1908
26/7/47	1716
26/3/49	1744
13/6/50	2246
2/9/52	2623
9/8/55	2739
29/4/60	2642
25/3/61	2255
8/3/62	2732

Mileage at 28/12/63 903,754
Withdrawn 21/7/65

6820 ex-works at Swindon shed and ready to go back to Worcester in the new lined green, 15 May 1960. The new diesels are an obvious presence. Alec Swain, transporttreasury

KINGSTONE GRANGE at Newton Abbot shed; unlined black, now with 4,000 gallon tender, 18 August 1957. Ken Fairey, ColourRail.

A Grange with a train of vans, as nature intended; 6820 KINGSTONE GRANGE with tall chimney, capuchon and 'intermediate' 3,500 gallon tender runs through Swindon on 10 June 1951. Typical oil leakage from the dart-shaped lubrication pipe cover above the steampipe. Norman Preedy Archive.

6821 LEATON GRANGE
Built January 1937

Mileages and Boilers

From new		7221
26/8/39	97,653	7221
6/10/42	197,217	7221
8/9/44	253,666	C2865
5/2/48	353,869	C7262
29/7/49	411,041	C2867
3/1/52	516,106	C4437
1/6/54	620,074	C4437
29/8/56	727,133	C2952
6/11/58	826,190	C2952
10/4/62	926,900	C7263

Sheds and Works

6/3/37	Canton
17/6/37	Hereford Shops **R**
2/7/37	Old Oak Shops **R**
26/8/39	Wolverhampton Works **I**
16/9/39	Ebbw Jct.
6/10/42	Swindon Works **I**
1/7/43	Ebbw Jct. Shed **R**
31/8/43	Ebbw Jct. Shops **R**
8/9/44	Swindon Works **HG**
12/6/45	Ebbw Jct. Shops **R**
27/10/45	Worcester Shops **R**
8/8/46	Gloucester Shops **R**
25/4/47	Ebbw Jct. Shed **R**
22/9/47	Ebbw Jct. Shed **R**
29/10/47	Hereford Shops **R**
17/12/47	Shrewsbury Shops **R**
5/2/48	Swindon Works **I**
29/7/49	Swindon Works **HG**
3/1/52	Swindon Works **HG**
23/3/52	Old Oak
1/11/52	Laira
21/3/53	Laira Shops **U**
1/6//54	Swindon Works **HI**
29/4/55	Laira Shops **U**
19/8/55	Newton Abbot Works **LC**
12/9/55	Laira Shops **U**
29/8/56	Swindon Works **HG**
22/3/58	Oxford
17/7/58	Ebbw Jct. Shops **U**
6/11/58	Swindon Works **HI**
13/3/59	Old Oak Shops **U**
28/11/59	Pontypool Road
30/4/61	Pontypool Road Shops **U**
17/6/61	Ebbw Jct.
29/6/61	Canton Shops **U**
9/9/61	Pontypool Road
10/4/62	Swindon Works **HG**
12/9/62	Ebbw Jct. Shops **U**
29/6/63	St. Philips Marsh
20/1/64	Worcester Shops **U**
22/6/64	Barrow Road
5/10/64	Llanelly

Tenders

From new	2029
6/10/42	1880
8/9/44	1682
15/2/48	2121
26/3/49	1716
29/7/49	2264
3/1/52	2833
1/6/54	2104
29/8/56	2260
6/11/58	2254
10/4/62	2772

Mileage at 28/12/63 975,981
Withdrawn 9/11/64

LEATON GRANGE approaching Wolverhampton Low Level with empty stock. The year is not known and there is no shed plate but 6821 has a 4,000 gallon tender (2772 from 4/62) and its cleanliness is very 1963-64; that is, lamentable. John Ashley, Michael Boakes Collection.

More vans. 6821 LEATON GRANGE heads a down train of them out of Victory Siding Loop near Wellington (Somerset) on 29 October 1953. Alan Lathey, transporttreasury

6822 MANTON GRANGE
Built January 1937

Mileages and Boilers

From new		7222
2/8/39	96,592	7222
31/8/42	206,329	C2829
16/7/46	315,592	C4460
12/4/49	385,185	C4460
26/9/51	471,354	C2931
25/6/53	541,727	C4069
23/12/55	645,169	C7266
22/5/58	738,932	C4485
23/2/61	836,867	C2870

Sheds and Works

6/3/37	Exeter
2/8/39	Swindon Factory **I**
3/1941	Newton Abbot
31/8/42	Swindon Factory **HG**
27/11/44	Newton Abbot Works **L**
16/4/45	Newton Abbot Works **L**
17/7/45	Swindon Factory **L**
16/7/46	Swindon Factory **I**
21/11/47	Newton Abbot Shed **R**
12/1/48	Newton Abbot Shed **R**
21/6/48	Newton Abbot Works **L**
	Tender work only
24/9/48	Newton Abbot Works **R**
12/4/49	Swindon Factory **HI**
10/5/51	Newton Abbot Works **U**
26/9/51	Swindon Factory **HI**
25/6/53	Swindon Factory **HG**
3/12/54	St Blazey Shops **U**
5/11/55	Westbury
23/12/55	Swindon Factory **I**
22/3/58	Oxford
22/5/58	Swindon Factory **HG**
3/12/59	Old Oak Shops **U**
30/1/60	Canton
23/2/61	Swindon Factory **HG**
31/5/61	Carmarthen Shops **U**
19/11/61	Aberdare Shops **LC**
21/6/62	Caerphilly Works **LC**
8/9/62	Cardiff, East Dock
17/11/62	Pontypool Road
28/2/63	Pontypool Road Shops **U**
21/4/64	Aberdare Shops **U**
22/6/64	Barrow Road

Tenders

From new	2328
2/8/39	2161
31/8/42	2881
16/7/46	2037
12/7/48	2355
25/6/53	2261
23/12/55	2906
22/5/58	2251
23/2/61	1838
12/1962	2349

Mileage at 28/12/63 918,103
Withdrawn 28/9/64

Alongside the coaling stage at Bristol Bath Road. The print is not dated but it is in the engine's Newton Abbot (83A) days; it is in plain black with the first emblem so it might well be a short while after its Heavy General at Swindon in 1953 – the tender record suits this perfectly. ColourRail.

6822 MANTON GRANGE at its home shed, Newton Abbot, in the early 1950s; low-sided tender. There was certainly a profusion of nuts and rivets on a Grange front end... The little protruding plates on the curved front plates are clear, along with the bolts in place of rivets, where panels were removed to aid the job of valve removal. In June 1949 MANTON GRANGE had been the engine used in clearance tests between Exeter Central and Templecombe, hauling one SR brake composite coach, stopping at all stations and returning the following day after spending the night at Yeovil shed. It turned out that platform clearances at Sidmouth Junction and Chard Junction were insufficient for Granges to be used regularly. J. Davenport, Initial Photographics.

6823 OAKLEY GRANGE

Built January 1937

Sheds and Works

6/3/37	Goodwick
23/7/38	Swindon Works
1/4/39	Swindon Works **I**
3/1941	Swindon Works
11/5/42	Swindon Works **I**
25/5/44	Swindon Works **HG**
15/6/46	Swindon Works
24/1/48	Swindon Works
21/5/49	Swindon Works **HG**
27/1/51	Worcester Shops
23/7/51	Swindon Works **HG**
1/11/52	Ebbw Jct.
21/2/53	Swindon
21/3/53	Swindon Works
18/4/53	Stourbridge
18/2/54	Swindon Works **HG**
8/10/55	Chester
6/7/56	Swindon Works **HI**
5/10/57	Banbury
26/4/58	Banbury Shops **U**
14/6/58	Laira
27/6/58	Laira Shops **U**
1/11/58	Truro
22/11/58	Swindon Works **HG**
7/10/61	Oxley
Oxley transferred to LMR 1/1/63	

Mileages and Boilers

21/1/37		7223
21/4/39	93,512	7223
13/6/42	196,986	7223
6/7/44	267,620	7208
29/7/46	336,698	4487
30/5/49	447,397	4055
22/8/51	520,561	9298
23/3/54	611,897	4426
24/8/56	686,617	9203
8/1/59	770,614	2954
3/5/62	872,615	7232

Tenders

From new	1983
21/4/39	2021
13/6/42	2325
29/7/46	2076
26/2/48	2219
4/9/48	1986
30/5/49	2328
22/8/51	2251
4/10/52	1983
19/3/53	2638
23/4/54	2827
14/1/56	2265
11/10/58	2597
8/1/59	2736
3/5/62	2674

Mileage at 28/12/63 922,338
Withdrawn 6/65

A glistening Grange in the snow, fully overhauled and ready for the light up and first tentative run, at Swindon; 4,000 gallon tender. There is no date but this is surely OAKLEY GRANGE's Heavy General of November 1958; the lined green and second emblem rule out anything earlier and yes, it did snow in England that November in 1958! Norman Preedy Archive.

6823 OAKLEY GRANGE at Laira shed on 27 June 1960; a Truro engine, it had been based at all the far reaches of the system – far Wales, far West, far Midlands! 5069 ISAMBARD KINGDOM BRUNEL in the background. Norman Preedy Archive.

By now an Oxley engine, at Severn Tunnel Junction shed in straitened circumstances. OAKLEY GRANGE was the engine involved in the curious accident near Fishguard and Goodwick in July 1951 – possibly the only one in history to be caused by a wedding party! In a head-on collision with 0-4-2T 1423, OAKLEY GRANGE with a goods suffered bent frames and 'badly distorted' buffer beams. The 0-4-2T with an auto train had left the station without the train staff and passed the starting signal at danger. A railwayman's wedding party was departing close by and 1423's driver had been distracted by the explosion of numerous detonators and the whistling of locos in the nearby engine shed. Only the auto driver was hurt enough to be detained in hospital. The Inspector was aware, you feel, of appearing too po-faced but had to point out the improper use of detonators, a custom at weddings that was not confined to Fishguard by any means. 'Everyone would wish to show goodwill on such occasions' Brigadier Langley wrote but instructions, he reported 'had now been issued to prohibit the light-hearted abuse of these valuable safeguards...' J. Davenport, Initial Photographics.

6824 ASHLEY GRANGE
Built January 1937

Mileages and Boilers
Date	Mileage	Boiler
From new		7224
14/9/40	104,697	C7224
17/5/43	203,588	C7224
31/1/45	277,166	C4091
5/12/47	395,624	C8254
26/6/50	497,706	C2890
17/2/53	600,095	C8227
18/5/55	700,877	C8227
16/7/57	793,056	C8280
26/1/60	908,911	C4422
4/3/63	992,607	C9220

Sheds and Works
3/4/37	Llanelly
24/8/38	Llanelly Shops **L**
11/5/39	Swindon Works **L**
1/2/40	Swindon Works **L**
14/9/40	Swindon Works **I**
7/1941	Carmarthen
29/4/42	Aberdare Shops **R**
29/5/42	Carmarthen Shops **L**
17/5/43	Swindon Works **I**
31/4/45	Swindon Works **HG**
13/6/46	Carmarthen Shops **L**
30/5/47	Cheltenham Shops **R**
5/12/47	Swindon Works **I**
23/4/49	Llanelly
7/3/50	Llanelly Shops **U**
26/6/50	Swindon Works **HG**
26/1/52	Penzance
19/1/53	Swindon Works **HG**
18/5/55	Wolverhampton Works **HI**
11/6/56	Penzance Shops **U**
16/7/57	Swindon Works **HG**
9/1/59	Newton Abbot Shops **U**
26/1/60	Swindon Works **HI**
29/3/62	Penzance Shops **U**
7/8/62	Penzance Shops **U**
11/8/62	Laira
6/10/62	Didcot
4/3/63	Swindon Works **HG**
16/5/63	Swindon Works **U**
2/11/63	Oxford

Tenders
Date	Tender
From new	1996
11/5/39	2015
1/2/40	1947
14/9/40	2103
17/5/43	1697
29/6/46	2158
3/7/46	2125
5/12/47	2015
26/6/50	2077
17/2/53	2266
4/6/57	2687
26/1/60	2657
4/3/63	2835

Mileage at 28/12/63 1,014,032
Withdrawn 8/4/64

6824 ASHLEY GRANGE looking good on the approach roads to Penzance shed; with tail lamp on it will be about to back down to the terminus. The year would probably be 1960; the shed is in the background with one of the new D6300 Type 2s outside the Repair Shop, now an impromptu diesel shop. A. Robey, transporttreasury

Now a Didcot engine, at Old Oak Common on 30 July 1963; larger cover on boiler/smokebox above the ejector pipe indicating increased superheating.

6825 LLANVAIR GRANGE
Built February 1937

Mileages and Boilers
Date	Mileage	Boiler
From new		7225
10/6/39	95,160	7225
26/2/42	197,594	C4487
3/3/45	297,385	C7261
18/8/48	403,047	C4477
4/7/50	492,908	C2847
31/7/52	582,394	C2871
11/6/54	669,961	C4073
16/4/56	754,585	C4073
18/7/58	851,565	C6214
5/10/61	957,558	C9284

Sheds and Works
3/4/37	Exeter
10/6/39	Swindon Works I
4/1940	Penzance
25/7/40	Penzance Shops R
15/11/40	Penzance Shops R
8/4/41	Newton Abbot Works L
10/9/41	Penzance Shops R
26/2/42	Swindon Works HG
22/10/42	Penzance Shops R
22/4/43	Penzance Shops L
22/8/43	Penzance Shops R
23/10/43	Penzance Shops R
28/11/43	Penzance Shops R
12/1943	Newton Abbot
13/2/44	Newton Abbot Shed L
14/6/44	Newton Abbot Shed R
3/3/45	Swindon Works I
29/11/45	Newton Abbot Works L
23/2/46	Penzance
4/4/46	Penzance Shops R
30/9/46	Penzance shops R
10/1/47	Newton Abbot Works L
25/5/47	Penzance Shops R
3/7/47	Newton Abbot Works L
31/10/47	Penzance Shops R
27/2/48	Penzance Shops R
18/8/48	Swindon Works I
23/5/49	Penzance Shops U
19/1/50	Newton Abbot Works U
4/7/50	Swindon Works HG
1/2/51	Newton Abbot Works U
24/5/51	Newton Abbot works LC
7/11/51	Penzance Shops
31/7/52	Swindon Works HI
11/6/54	Swindon Works HG
16/4/56	Newton Abbot Works HI
2/4/57	St. Blazey Shops U
18/7/58	Swindon Works HG
6/8/60	Penzance Shops U
5/10/61	Swindon Factory HG
8/10/61	St. Blazey
4/11/61	Penzance
14/7/62	Laira
6/10/62	Reading
4/5/64	St Philip's Marsh
30/5/64	Worcester Shops U

Tenders
Date	Tender
From new	2219
24/1/42	2698
26/2/42	2227
22/4/43	2350
3/3/45	2894
18/8/48	2242
8/10/48	1952
31/7/52	1639
18/5/57	2872
5/10/61	2261

Mileage to 28/12/63 1,019,472
Withdrawn 15/6/64, Sold to Birds, Risca 18/8/64

6825 LLANVAIR GRANGE in black with no tender emblem, on a goods at Truro. 'Llanvair' was the anglicised version of the name, 6877 carrying the proper Welsh 'Llanfair', a little absurdly. J. Davenport, Initial Photographics.

LLANVAIR GRANGE outside the Repair Shop at Penzance shed (stores van behind) more or less where the D6300 diesel is in the picture of 6824. This picture (unlike the one by Jim Davenport at Truro) is dated 1958 and it is pretty safe to assume that this picture too, dates from 1958 or earlier; the loco underwent a Heavy General later in the year and came out in lined green with the second emblem. Michael Boakes Collection.

6825 and 6824 at Penzance shed, Good Friday 1962. J.L. Stevenson, courtesy Hamish Stevenson.

6826 NANNERTH GRANGE
Built February 1937

Mileages and Boilers

Date	Mileage	Boiler
From new		7226
16/3/39	101,647	7226
31/1/42	210,820	7226
27/4/45	321,436	C7224
18/1/47	403,697	C2867
29/6/49	483,560	C4043
31/8/51	576,883	R9299
15/12/53	688,003	R9299
26/2/56	780,820	C4471
2/7/59	889,361	C7222
24/11/61	1,014,565	C6209

Sheds and Works

1/5/37	Old Oak
16/3/39	Swindon Works **I**
31/1/42	Swindon Works **I**
31/3/44	Old Oak Shops **R**
22/7/44	Westbury Shops **R**
29/8/44	Laira Shops **R**
2/12/44	Old Oak Shed **R**
27/4/45	Swindon Works **HG**
6/7/46	Southall Shops **R**
13/7/46	Southall
18/1/47	Swindon Works **HI**
11/8/47	Southall Shops **R**
28/2/48	Southall Shops **R**
20/8/48	Wolverhampton Works **R**
29/6/49	Swindon Works **HG**
3/12/49	Penzance
31/3/50	Truro Shops **U**
16/10/50	Penzance Shops **U**
23/1/51	Penzance Shops **U**
31/8/51	Swindon Works **HG**
6/11/52	Penzance Shops **U**
15/12/53	Swindon Works **HI**
28/2/56	Swindon Works **HG**
12/2/57	Laira Shops **U**
3/5/58	Penzance Shops **U**
2/7/58	Swindon Works **HG**
2/10/59	Newton Abbot Works **LC**
24/11/61	Swindon Works **HG**
14/7/62	Laira
6/10/62	Reading
5/5/64	Cardiff East Dock

Tenders

Date	Tender
From new	2206
16/3/39	1921
31/1/42	2328
18/1/47	1876
29/6/49	1733
31/8/51	2244
15/12/53	2657
26/2/56	1838
22/2/58	1910
2/7/58	2782
24/11/61	2871

Mileage at 28/12/63 1,072,575
Withdrawn 7/5/65

6826 NANNERTH GRANGE coming into Penzance in the summer of 1957. It had been one of those wartime Southall Granges but soon came to the West where it stayed until the clearout of steam, finding itself back in the London Division at Reading. Low-sided tender. Norman Preedy Archive.

Good Friday 1962 (see 6825 with 6824 earlier) and the diesels are firmly established at Penzance shed; 4,000 gallon tender. J.L. Stevenson, courtesy Hamish Stevenson.

NANNERTH GRANGE, at Gloucester Horton Road, in July 1964. Michael Boakes Collection.

6827 LLANFRECHFA GRANGE

Built February 1937

Mileages and Boilers

From new		7227
4/8/39	96,569	7227
24/1/42	186,558	7227
2/9/44	282,089	C4406
5/7/47	395,913	C7210
26/1/50	488,406	C2954
14/5/52	571,449	C4980
24/9/54	670,744	C2938
21/3/57	755,238	C2938
31/12/59	846,264	C6206
28/3/62	924,345	C2844

Sheds and Works

3/4/37	Truro
5/3/38	Newton Abbot Works **L**
15/10/38	Penzance
12/11/38	Newton Abbot Works **L**
24/6/39	Swindon Factory **I**
19/8/39	Canton
12/12/41	Swindon Works **I**
12/5/43	Canton Shops **R**
14/4/44	Canton, Shops **R**
1/8/44	Swindon Works **HG**
7/12/45	Newton Abbot Works **L**
23/3/46	Swindon Works **L**
2/6/47	Swindon Works **I**
15/5/48	St Philips Marsh
24/1/49	Bristol Shops **U**
23/7/49	Hereford Shops **U**
3/12/49	Swindon Works **HG**
19/1/51	Old Oak Shed **U**
15/4/52	Swindon Works **HI**
16/5/53	Truro
3/10/53	St Philips Marsh
24/8/54	Swindon Works **HG**
2/12/55	Taunton Shops **U**
3/4/56	St. Philips Marsh Shops **U**
21/12/56	St. Philips Marsh Shops **U**
18/2/57	Wolverhampton Works **HI**
7/8/58	Exeter Shops **U**
31/11/59	Swindon Works **HG**
16/5/61	Ebbw Jct. Shops **U**
12/2/62	Swindon Works **HI**
31/8/62	Worcester Shops **U**
6/10/62	Stourbridge
18/4/64	Oxley

Oxley transferred to LMR 1/1/63

Tenders

From new	2204
8/28	2125
4/8/39	2241
24/1/42	2568
2/9/44	2354
12/4/46	1929
29/12/45	1989
26/1/46	1959
23/2/46	2003
25/3/46	2204
25/1/47	2008
8/4/47	2872
26/1/50	1972
14/9/52	2737
31/12/59	2666
30/12/61	2609
5/3/62	2254

Mileage to 31/12/62, 967,876
Withdrawn 25/9/65

6827 LLANFRECHFA GRANGE in black, at Exeter St David's with the 8.10am Manchester (London) August 1955. W. Hermiston, transporttreasury

6827 LLANFRECHFA GRANGE in black, at Exeter St David's with the 8.10am Penzance to Manchester (London Road) on 6 August 1955. W. Hermiston, transporttreasury

6828 TRELLECH GRANGE
Built February 1937

Mileages and Boilers
Date	Mileage	Boiler
From new		7228
4/9/40	102,772	7228
12/4/43	192,628	R9219
30/8/45	280,672	C8292
26/8/47	364,624	C2939
16/9/49	444,544	C2908
29/11/50	487,615	C4076
6/6/52	537,616	C4076
28/7/54	599,949	C7227
20/10/55	636,479	C7727
12/11/57	698,399	C8256
9/6/61	810,625	C7218

Sheds and Works
1/5/37	Landore
2/4/38	Llanelly
13/7/39	Swindon Works **L**
19/12/39	Swindon Works **L**
4/9/40	Swindon Works **I**
18/7/41	Swindon Works **L**
12/4/43	Swindon Works **HG**
30/8/45	Swindon Works **L**
3/7/47	Laira shops **R**
26/8/47	Swindon Works **I**
17/4/48	Llanelly
12/6/48	Stourbridge
29/6/49	Stourbridge Shops **U**
16/9/49	Swindon Works **HG**
26/3/50	Stourbridge Shops **U**
9/10/50	Stourbridge Shops **U**
29/11/50	Swindon Works **HC**
4/1/52	Stourbridge Shops **U**
6/6/52	Swindon Works **HI**
11/10/52	Stourbridge Shops **U**
27/8/53	Stourbridge Shops **U**
15/6/54	Swindon Works **HC**
11/9/55	Stourbridge Shops **U**
20/10/55	Swindon Works **HI**
13/7/57	Llanelly
5/10/57	Landore
12/11/57	Caerphilly Works **HG**
22/3/58	Llanelly
23/9/58	Caerphilly Works **U**
29/11/58	Truro
14/7/59	Newton Abbot Works **U**
9/6/61	Swindon Works **HI**
7/10/61	Oxley
29/8/62	Oswestry Works **U**

Tenders
Date	Tender
From new	2161
13/7/39	1880
19/12/39	2034
4/9//40	1947
12/4/43	2068
30/8/45	2897
26/8/47	2876
26/3/50	2357
9/10/50	2834
29/11/50	2908
6/6/52	2249
15/6/54	2265
20/10/55	2642
6/9/59	2571
9/6/61	2607
12/62	2097

Final recorded mileage 875,150
Withdrawn 23/7/63
According to BR9215 form cut up w/e 27/9/63
GWR history sheet gives date as 5/10/63

6828 TRELLECH GRANGE at Chester shed, 22 July 1951. The engine has the earlier tapered buffers, as does 5027 beyond; later a parallel type was used. R.C. Riley, transporttreasury

6828's last proper overhaul, a Heavy Intermediate, at Swindon on 28 May 1961. L.W. Rowe, ColourRail.

The contrast to the grime of Chester could not be more marked. In scintillating lined green 6828 stands on Swindon shed in June 1961. J. Davenport, Initial Photographics.

6829 BURMINGTON GRANGE
Built March 1937

Mileages and Boilers

Date	Mileage	Boiler
From new		7229
9/6/39	92,554	7229
19/8/41	169,216	7229
12/1/44	254,736	2967
12/3/47	375,393	C8257
14/9/49	447,018	C4441
11/2/52	529,891	R6205
21/10/54	637,849	C8265
11/4/57	733,784	C2842
24/9/59	834,620	C6211
21/9/62	926,898	C6219

Sheds and Works

1/5/37	Truro
13/4/38	Newton Abbot Works L
29/11/38	Newton Abbot Works L
10/12/38	Penzance
9/6/39	Swindon Works I
26/6/40	Penzance Shops R
17/10/40	Penzance Shops R
13/2/41	Newton Abbot Works L
10/4/41	Taunton Shops R
24/5/41	Penzance Shops R
19/8/41	Swindon Works I
10/1941	Truro
27/2/42	Newton Abbot Works L
24/9/42	Penzance Shops R
20/1/43	Newton Abbot Works L
2/6/43	Newton Abbot Works R
29/9/43	Truro Shops R
12/1/44	Swindon Works HG
20/3/45	Truro Shops R
4/5/45	Swindon Works L
7/5/45	Swindon Works I Tender repair
26/10/45	Truro Shops R
12/3/47	Swindon Works I
16/4/48	Newton Abbot Works L Tender work only
29/6/48	Newton Abbot Shed R
14/9/49	Swindon Works HG
By 6/50	Newton Abbot
11/2/52	Swindon Works HG
18/5/53	Newton Abbot works U
21/10/54	Swindon Works HI
5/1/56	Newton Abbot works LC
11/4/57	Swindon Works HG
18/3/59	Old Oak Shops U
24/9/59	Swindon Works HI
21/5/60	Exeter
8/10/60	Ebbw Jct.
31/3/61	Ebbw Jct. Shops U
10/5/62	Ebbw Jct. Shops U
21/9/62	Swindon Works HG
18/6/64	Pontypool Road
2/6/64	Barrow Road
10/7/65	Worcester

Tenders

Date	Tender
From new	2350
19/841	2204
12/1/44	2355
10/7/48	2037
14/9/49	2334
11/2/52	2787
21/10/54	2923
11/4/57	2256
24/9/59	2264
21/9/62	2813

Mileage at 28/12/63 968,543
Withdrawn 18/11/65

6829 BURMINGTON GRANGE at the summit of Dainton at the entry to the west facing mouth of the tunnel. The summit itself is inside the tunnel when in each direction there is a sharp change of gradient, like a gable on a building. The year is 1953 in late summer – notice the 'stooks' in the field. In Devon this would be middle to late August. The train is an up stopper, that may become a Class A train for Bristol and the Midlands from Exeter St David's. The load looks to be the maximum for an eastbound train unassisted. The dating is fixed by the original signal box which was destroyed by fire later in the 1950s. Behind the box is a banking spur with a 51XX 2-6-2T that has banked a westbound goods, and is waiting a path back to Newton. The other sidings were put in to serve the by now defunct Dainton quarry. Peter Townend.

Tall chimney, capuchon-less on the 3.15 pm Acton-Hackney Yard goods (often worked by 4700 2-8-0s until 1963) approaching the 'North Circular' bridge on 29 August 1963 at Hanger Lane. The bridge in the background carries the Piccadilly Line to Uxbridge; the Tube lines to the left are those of the Central Line. Peter Groom.

6830 BUCKENHILL GRANGE
Built August 1937

Sheds and Works
124/8/37	Ebbw
18/9/37	Pontypool Road
6/10/39	Swindon Works **I**
11/11/39	Westbury
9/1940	Swindon Works
15/12/42	Swindon Works **I**
1/1944	St Philips Marsh
23/4/45	Swindon Works **HG**
7/1945	Bath Road
20/4/46	St Philips Marsh
12/7/47	Swindon Works **I**
3/12/49	Swindon Works **HC**
26/1/52	Swindon Works **HG**
16/5/53	Caerphilly Works
6/11/54	Swindon Works **HI**
18/2/57	Swindon Works **HG**
25/2/58	Newton Abbot Shops
12/2/60	Swindon Works **HG**
27/1/62	Penzance
21/4/62	Oxley
6/11/63	Wolverhampton Works **R**

Tenders
From new	2172
1940	1986
1942	2015
1946	2903
1950	2220
1952	2906 2434
1956	2832
1958	2255 [23/4/57]
1960	2832
1962	2905

NO FURTHER DETAIL

Withdrawn 9/10/65

6830 BUCKENHILL GRANGE at Taunton with a train for Bristol and Cardiff, 8 August 1955. J. Robertson, transporttreasury

At Didcot about 1962-63, after 4,000 gallon tender attached. J. Davenport, Initial Photographics.

6831 BEARLEY GRANGE
Built August 1937

Sheds and Works
24/8/37	Banbury
5/1/40	Wolverhampton Works **I**
21/2/40	Stafford Road
4/1940	Tyseley
3/1942	Tyseley Shops
14/9/43	Swindon Works **I**
3/5/45	Swindon Works **HG**
25/1/47	Tyseley Shops
22/10/47	Swindon Works **I**
27/1148	Leamington Spa
24/1/49	Tyseley
21/2/49	Birkenhead
20/5/50	Swindon Works **HG**
27/12/52	Swindon Works **HG**
17/11/55	Swindon Works **HI**
3/2/56	Wolverhampton Works **U**
20/5/58	St Philips Marsh
13/10/58	Swindon Works **HC**
30/5/61	Swindon Works **HI**
27/1/62	Penzance
21/4/62	Oxley
22/12/63	Swindon Works **HG**

Tenders
From new	2007
1940	2057
1946	2015
1948	1904
1952	2245 [16/5/50]
1954	2433
1958	2259 [13/10/58]
1962	2917

Withdrawn 16/10/65

A smoke-laden 6831 BEARLEY GRANGE at Bristol's Stapleton Road station in September 1960; it has an 'intermediate' 3,500 gallon tender and is just about as filthy as a loco can get. ColourRail.

BEARLEY GRANGE slogs through Wellington, Shropshire, 7 September 1963. L.W. Rowe, ColourRail.

Glorious in green on 23 July 1961, a lined 6831 stands at Swindon works, alongside the surviving Dean Goods 0-6-0, 2516 later preserved. With lined livery, second emblem and electrification flashes this is just after its Heavy overhaul of May-June 1961. Ray Hinton Archive, courtesy Norman Preedy.

6832 BROCKTON GRANGE

Built August 1937

Mileages and Boilers

From new		2982
1/3/40	90,666	2982
4/10/42	167,493	2982
17/6/44	214,613	C4063
29/1/46	263,288	C4993
9/6/48	343,843	C2809
5/10/50	425,584	C2928
29/7/53	532,074	C2928
5/1/56	613,823	C2855
4/12/58	719,969	C4938
10/10/61	804,447	C8231

Sheds and Works

18/9/37	Tyseley
1/3/40	Swindon Works **I**
5/3/40	Leamington Spa
5/1940	Banbury
17/7/40	Swindon Works **L**
1/1/41	Swindon Works Tender work only
4/10/42	Swindon Works **I**
2/12/42	Banbury Shops **L**
4/10/43	Banbury Shops **R**
17/6/44	Swindon Works **L**
25/8/45	Bath Road Shops **R**
29/1/46	Swindon Works **HG**
4/9/47	Banbury Shops **R**
9/6/48	Swindon Works **I**
29/11/49	Banbury Shops **U**
3/12/49	St Philips Marsh
5/10/50	Swindon Works **HG**
1/11/52	Swindon
12/3/53	Westbury Shops
29/7/53	Swindon Works **HI**
10/2/55	Swindon shed **U**
5/1/56	Swindon Works **HG**
15/10/56	Swindon shed **U**
2/11/56	Old Oak Shops **U**
28/12/57	St Blazey
4/12/58	Swindon Works **HG**
4/10/58	Laira
By 3/59	Truro
28/11/59	Canton
18/12/59	Caerphilly Works **LC**
18/6/60	Llanelly
14/7/60	Canton Shops **U**
4/8/60	Canton Shops **U**
8/9/60	Caerphilly Works **U**
10/10/61	Swindon Works **HG**
4/11/61	Neath
1/8/62	Neath Shops **U**
By 2/63	Llanelly

Tenders

From new	2003
5/3/40	2355
17/7/40	2354
4/10/42	2108
14/6/47	1795
18/5/48	1838
9/6/48	1777
17/6/50	1720
5/10/50	2003
21/8/52	2135
29/7/53	2635
5/1/56	2261
10/10/61	2242

Mileage at 28/12/63 870,104
Withdrawn 15/1/64, Sold to G. Cohen, Morriston, 24/3/64

6832 BROCKTON GRANGE on Swindon shed, 6 May 1956; 'intermediate' tender. A.R. Carpenter, transporttreasury

In fine fettle and now in lined green, the tender though still 'intermediate' has the second emblem (small size) and is loaded with the detested 'cobbles'. The location is Over Junction, Gloucester in March 1963 and BROCKTON GRANGE has a long train of vans from South Wales. Telford's bridge in the background carries the A48 main road to South Wales. Norman Preedy.

6833 CALCOT GRANGE
Built August 1937

Sheds and Works
18/9/37	Oxley
1/4/39	Tyseley
23/1/40	Swindon Works **I**
10/1/43	Swindon Works **HG**
6/1944	Tyseley Shops
10/1944	Tyseley Shops
17/5/46	Swindon Works **I**
10/7/48	Swindon Works
10/9/49	Leamington Spa
7/10/50	Swindon Works **HG**
1/12/51	Banbury
14/6/52	Chester
18/2/53	Swindon Works **HI**
19/6/54	St Philips Marsh
10/9/55	Swindon Works **HG**
16/10/58	Wolverhampton Works **HI**
23/9/59	St. Philips Marsh Shops **U**
27/1/60	Canton
23/11/60	Swindon Works **HG**
24/2/62	Penzance
19/5/62	Oxley
4/3/63	Wolverhampton Works **U**
6/5/63	Wolverhampton Works **U**
15/9/63	Swindon Works **HG**

Tenders
From new	2358
1940	2485 1728
19144	2358
1946	2890
1948	1838
1950	2045
1952	2642
1954	2422 2346
1956	2243 [14/10/51]
1960	2246 [11/1/61]
1964	2540

Withdrawn 16/10/65

CALCOT GRANGE by the coal stage at Oxley shed (late home to many Granges) on 8 August 1963. The Great Train Robbery had taken place a few hours before... Hamish Stevenson.

6833 CALCOT GRANGE before the War; GWR art deco roundel, plain green livery and vacuum pump lubricator on running plate by leading splasher, old style tapered buffers. transporttreasury

6834 DUMMER GRANGE
Built August 1937

Sheds and Works
18/9/37	Severn Tunnel Jct.
9/12/39	Wolverhampton Works **I**
27/1/40	Oxley
3/1940	Severn Tunnel Jct.
22/8/42	Swindon Works **I**
3/1944	Newton Abbot Works
22/3/45	Swindon Works **HG**
1/11/47	Swindon Works **I**
12/6/48	Pontypool Road
30/10/48	Ebbw Jct.
5/5/50	Swindon Works **HG**
23/3/52	Old Oak
1/11/52	Reading
29/11/52	Swindon Works **HG**
16/7/55	Oxford
5/11/55	Swindon Works **HI**
31/12/55	Laira
8/9/56	St Philips Marsh
17/4/58	Swindon Works **HG**
4/8/61	Swindon Works **HI**
6/10//62	Southall
6/4/63	Reading
18/4/64	Stourbridge

Tenders
From new	2108
1942	2219
1946	2321
1948	1744
1950	2227 2266 [5/6/50]
1954	2582
1956	2257 [4/11/55]
12/10/61-7/64	2258

Withdrawn 6/64

Lined and green at St Philips Marsh; the 82B plate tells us the period is 1956-1962. J. Davenport, Initial Photographics.

6834 DUMMER GRANGE plain and unadorned in black; 'intermediate' 3,500 gallon tender; there is no date or location available but prime suspect is Ebbw Junction. J.T. Clewley, transporttreasury

6835 EASTHAM GRANGE

Built September 1937

Mileages and Boilers
Date	Mileage	Boiler
From new		4041
2/3/40	88,574	4041
4/11/42	162,326	4041
6/6/44	204,619	C2834
4/4/46	263,205	C4971
20/12/48	360,883	C4957
3/4/51	433,851	C2860
2/2/53	501,616	C2804
6/7/55	597,832	C2804
22/8/57	678,108	C4070
26/5/60	782,907	C4028

Sheds and Works
18/9/37	Oxley
10/12/38	Stafford Road
18/1/40	Wolverhampton Works **I**
3/1940	Leamington Spa
6/1940	Banbury
1/6/40	Banbury Shops **R**
9/1/41	Ebbw Jct. Shops **L**
4/8/42	Swindon Works **I**
6/8/43	Old Oak Shops **R**
15/10/43	Banbury Shops **R**
6/6/44	Swindon Works **L**
30/11/44	Banbury Shops **R**
5/3/45	Stourbridge Shops **R**
18/8/45	Banbury Shops **R**
4/4/46	Swindon Works **I**
13/4/48	Banbury Shops **R**
13/9/48	Bath Road Shops **R**
20/12/48	Swindon Works **HG**
3/4/51	Swindon Works **HG**
14/6/52	Chester
17/12/52	Pontypool Road Shops **U**
2/2/53	Swindon Works **HG**
28/11/53	Tyseley
26/12/53	Chester
24/5/54	Chester Shops **U**
19/6/54	St. Philips Marsh
6/7/55	Swindon Works **HI**
19/10/56	St. Philips Marsh Shops **U**
22/8/57	Swindon Works **HG**
27/6/58	St. Philips Marsh Shops **U**
14/5/59	St. Philips Marsh Shops **U**
26/5/60	Swindon Works **HG**
10/8/60	Taunton Shops **U**
27/1/62	Penzance
22/2/62	Penzance Shops **U**
21/4/62	Oxley
19/5/62	St. Philips Marsh
14/6/62	Tyseley Shops **U**
18/6/62	Tyseley Shops **U**

Tenders
Date	Tender
From new	1801
4/11/42	2899
6/6/44	1750
20/12/48	1983
3/4/51	2699
2/2/53	2245
6/7/55	2616
22/8/57	2713
29/4/59	1898
26/5/60	2871

Final mileage 869,714
Withdrawn 20/5/63 Cut up 30/11/63

6835 EASTHAM GRANGE at Penzance shed with another Grange, 15 April 1962. These were the last months of steam in the far West and by September it had effectively been extinguished. Norman Preedy Archive.

6835 EASTHAM GRANGE looking splendid in lined green in Laira shed yard, 4 June 1960, only days out of a Heavy General at Swindon but predating the application of electrification flashes. The 'flashes' began appearing on WR locos around this time but only with any frequency in the following year, 1961. Peter Groom.

6836 ESTEVARNEY GRANGE

Built September 1937

Mileages and Boilers
Date	Mileage	Boiler
From new		4042
15/1/40	96,193	4042
25/4/42	173,413	4042
2/7/44	242,525	C2947
18/3/47	339,621	C2849
17/3/49	416,083	C8233
27/10/50	471,380	C2970
9/4/52	521,872	C2845
26/11/54	628,007	R6224
14/6/57	735,561	C6216
22/1/60	841,239	C8204
7/12/62	941,008	C6217

Sheds and Works
18/9/37	St. Philips Marsh
26/4/39	St. Philips Marsh Shops **R**
15/1/40	Swindon Works **I**
31/8/41	St. Philips Marsh Shops **R**
25/4/42	Swindon Works **I**
23/11/42	Newton Abbot Works **R**
23/5/45	Westbury Shops **R**
2/7/44	Swindon Works **HG**
18/3/47	Swindon Works **I**
27/1/48	Bath Road Shops **L** Tender work only
27/3/48	Bath Road Shops **L**
17/3/49	Swindon Works **HG**
3/2/50	St. Philips Marsh Shops **U**
27/10/50	Swindon Works **HC**
19/1/51	Wolverhampton Works **LC**
9/4//52	Swindon Works **HI**
16/5/53	Penzance
31/10/53	Carmarthen
26/12/53	Penzance
20/1/54	Laira Shops **LC**
26/11/54	Swindon Works **HG**
13/8/55	Newton Abbot
14/6/57	Swindon Works **HG**
22/1/60	Swindon Works **HI**
21/5/60	Laira
4/11/61	Pontypool Road
13/4/62	Pontypool Road Shops **U**
7/12/62	Swindon Works **HI**
3/3/64	Ebbw Jct. Shops **U**
22/6/64	Worcester

Tenders
Date	Tender
From new	1968
15/1/40	2015
25/4/42	1986
23/11/42	2125
2/7/44	2038
20/12/48	1951
17/3/49	1750
27/10/50	2254
19/1/51	2670
19/452	2819
14/6/57	2822
22/1/60	2555
4/3/61	2268
7/12/62	2827

Mileage at 28/12/63 977,638
Withdrawn 6/8/65

6836 ESTEVARNEY GRANGE at Laira shed, 5 August 1954, in black; 4,000 gallon tender with no markings. J. Robertson, transporttreasury

Perfect backdrop for a now-lined green Grange; Penzance station on 22 July 1957. J. Davenport, Initial Photographics.

A few years later and a world away in maintenance and upkeep. Cleared out of the West with the rest of steam, 6836 spent its last years at Pontypool Road and Worcester. This location, at a guess, is Shrewsbury shed, about 1964. ColourRail.

6837 FORTHAMPTON GRANGE
Built September 1937

Mileages and Boilers
From new		4043
17/10/39	99,042	4043
12/10/42	196,114	4043
25/10/45	283,569	C7238
21/3/49	393,104	C8264
12/10/51	489,876	C4482
1/2/54	587,135	C2874
3/5/56	686,931	C2874
28/5/58	786,942	R6233
8/12/60	889,665	C9243
10/9/63	963,949	C6247

Sheds and Works
16/10/37	Truro
15/10/38	Laira
17/10/39	Swindon Works **I**
11/11/39	Ebbw Jct.
22/8/40	Ebbw Jct. Shops **L**
28/1/42	Ebbw Jct. Shops **L**
27/7/42	Ebbw Jct. Shops **L**
12/10//42	Swindon Works **I**
5/10/43	Ebbw Jct. Shops **R**
23/6/44	Old Oak Shops **R**
30/10/44	Hereford Shops **R**
23/8/45	Banbury Shops **R**
25/10/45	Swindon Works **HG**
31/10/46	Ebbw Jct. Shops **L**
1/4/47	Ebbw Jct. Shops **L**
29/8/47	Swindon Works **L**
4/3/48	Ebbw Jct. Shops **R**
15/5/48	St. Philips Marsh
4/11/48	Bath Road Shops **R**
21/3/49	Swindon Works **HG**
7/10/50	Pontypool Road
4/11/50	Canton
13/4/51	Canton Shops **U**
12/10/51	Swindon Works **HI**
1/11/52	Pontypool Road
29/11/52	Penzance
6/6/52	Neath Shops **U**
17/10/52	Ebbw Jct. Shops **U**
1/2/54	Swindon Works **HG**
20/3/56	Truro Shops **U**
3/5/56	Swindon Works **HI**
28/5/58	Swindon Works **HG**
21/5/60	Laira
11/8/60	Laira Shops **U**
8/10/60	Llanelly
8/12/60	Swindon Works **HI**
20/10/61	Caerphilly Works **LC**
6/1/62	Carmarthen Shops **U**
3/8/62	Carmarthen Shops **U**
10/9/63	Swindon Works **HI**
7/11/64	Cardiff East Dock

Tenders
From new	2002
17/10/39	2034
12/10/42	2029
18/9/44	2889
21/3/49	1663
12/10/51	2872
1/2/54	2824
3/5/56	1898
3/11/57	2562
19/4/58	2259
28/5/58	2409
8/12/60	2892

Mileage at 28/12/63 973,613
Withdrawn 21/7/65

6837 FORTHAMPTON GRANGE was in Cornwall for the first year or two of its life and spent the War in South Wales, moving back to England and returning to the West only in 1952. On 8 August 1955 it is on a down workmen's train near Lipson Junction. Alan Lathey, transporttreasury

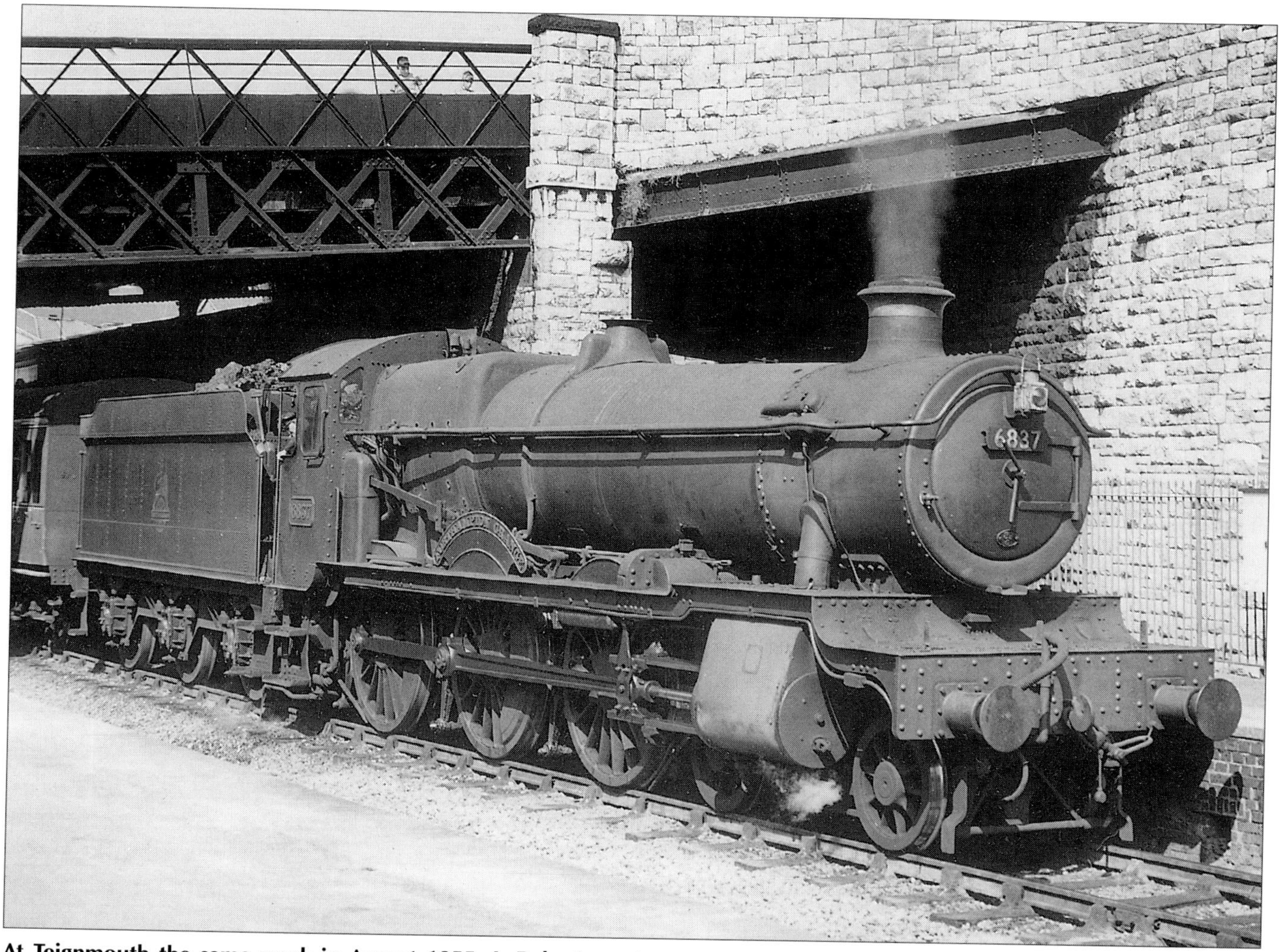

At Teignmouth the same week in August 1955. J. Robertson, transporttreasury

FORTHAMPTON GRANGE in late 1963, in good condition after a Heavy repair it is working vans through Cardiff General. Note – most unusually – no smokebox/boiler oil pipe cover this side. Norman Preedy Archive.

6838 GOODMOOR GRANGE

Built September 1937

Mileages and Boilers

From new		4044
18/4/40	91,702	4044
14/11/42	185,635	C4931
13/9/45	263,756	C7248
22/8/47	337,276	C8245
17/8/49	425,493	C8259
4/5/51	508,702	C4997
27/11/53	615,507	C4997
11/7/55	690,455	C2870
14/1/58	798,440	C2870
3/10/60	899,119	R6247
10/7/63	978,025	C9251

Sheds and Works

16/10/37	Chester
29/4/39	Tyseley
30/8/39	Tyseley Shops R
18/4/40	Swindon Works I
5/1940	Penzance
7/2/41	Newton Abbot Works R
16/10/41	Penzance Shops R
26/3/42	Newton Abbot Works L
12/8/42	Newton Abbot Works L
14/11/42	Swindon Works HG
28/7/43	Penzance Shops I
14/9/43	Penzance Shops R
8/12/43	Penzance Shops R
3/3/44	Penzance Shops R
2/6/44	Truro Shops R
6/7/44	Newton Abbot shops L
6/1/45	Penzance Shops R
24/3/45	Penzance Shops R
13/9/45	Swindon Works HG
3/12/46	Penzance hops R
12/2/47	Newton Abbot Works L
25/4/47	Penzance Shops R
4/6/47	Newton Abbot Works L
16/7/47	Newton Abbot Works L
22/8/47	Swindon Works I
30/12/47	Penzance Shops R
21/5/48	Newton Abbot Works L
	Tender work only
12/9/48	Penzance Shops R
10/2/49	Penzance Shops U
17/8/49	Swindon Works HG
4/5/51	Swindon Works HG
1/11/52	Laira
20/3/53	Laira Shops U
10/9/53	Laira Shops U
27/11/53	Swindon Works HI
25/6/54	Laira Shops U
13/12/54	Laira shops U
11/7/55	Swindon Works HG
8/9/56	Neyland
6/10/56	Ebbw Jct.
25/10/56	Taunton Shops U
11/6/57	Old Oak Shops U
14/1/58	Swindon Works HI
21/3/58	Caerphilly Works U
26/8/59	Ebbw Jct. Shops U
3/10/60	Swindon Works HG
3/10/60	Pontypool Road
10/10/62	Danygraig Shops U
20/12/62	Ebbw Jct. Shops U
24/2/63	Pontypool Road Shops U
10/7/63	Swindon Works HG
6/2/64	Pontypool Road Shops U
22/6/64	Barrow Road
13/6/64	Worcester Shops U
29/7/64	Llanelly
7/11/64	Cardiff East Dock
7/8/65	Worcester

Tenders

From new	1819
14/11/42	2900
13/9/45	1983
4/6/47	2876
22/8/47	2013
20/5/50	2038
24/2/52	2827
14/6/52	2069
13/6/53	1838
25/7/53	2367
27/11/53	2267
11/7/55	2107
14/1/58	2178
3/10/60	2800
10/7/63	2368

Mileage at 28/12/63 995,857
Withdrawn 18/11/65

It's a low-sided tender for 6838 years later, at Shrewsbury shed on 19 April 1964. 6874 HAUGHTON GRANGE alongside. It was withdrawn at the end of 1965 and may have had this tender till the end; no change is recorded, though odd in the final

6838 GOODMOOR GRANGE in pre-War condition; plain green with the roundel, low-sided tender, vacuum pump lubricator on running plate by leading splasher. W. Hermiston, transporttreasury

6839 HEWELL GRANGE
Built September 1937

Sheds and Works
16/10/37	Banbury
11/11/39	Swindon Works I
24/8/42	Swindon Works I
4/1944	Swindon Works
5/4/45	Swindon Works HG
27/12/47	Swindon Works I
22/4/50	Swindon Works HC
24/1/53	Wolverhampton Works HI
27/3/54	Wolverhampton Works
24/4/54	Oxley
8/1/55	Swindon Works HC
28/1/56	Swindon Works HG
3/1/58	Swindon Works HG
14/12/59	Swindon Works HG
31/12//60	Taunton
7/10/61	Oxley
9/1/62	Swindon Works HI

Tenders
From new	2095
1940	1880
1942	2897
1946	1797
1948	2321
1950	2268 [3/5/50]
1956	2789 2657
1960	2610
1962	2600

NO FURTHER DETAIL

Withdrawn 5/64

Below. 6839 HEWELL GRANGE at Saltney Junction on a down express, 19 June 1960. It's just come off the WR via the tracks crossing in front of the big signalbox and is heading towards Chester using (as all the down WR trains did) the up LMR slow lines from North Wales. From the shadows (the train is heading in a NE direction) the train itself is an afternoon departure from Paddington, arriving in Chester in the evening. The loco would have taken over from a King at Wolverhampton Low Level and the catering cars were taken off the train there too. The stock is pretty typical with a Hawksworth brake third and Mk1s, including a composite for the first class passengers; the fourth vehicle in the train. Typical that is apart from the trio of Gresley carriages tagged on to the rear (the middle one of which is an old, all-door type). These are almost certainly strengtheners, attached en route most probably (if they'd been attached in London they'd be at the front of the train.) It could well be that the train was strengthened at Wolverhampton during the loco change/removal of catering cars or even at Shrewsbury. Control would have advised those responsible that there were more passengers than seats on this service – what a wonderfully flexible railway we once ran! The extra trio will probably be taken off on arrival at Chester, leaving the remaining (service) carriages to be taken on to Birkenhead by a 2-6-4T. An up MR train is pegged alongside, it possibly heading *for* London as this one arrives *from* the capital. Both of Crane Street's distants are off so it should be a clear run into the General for both trains. The signal for the WR line to Wrexham carries the distant for the first box in Saltney yard. All the visible home signals are Saltney Junction's.
S. D. Wainwright.

6849 HEWELL GRANGE alongside the shed at Banbury, in June 1954. It still carries the vacuum pump lubricator on the running plate by the leading splasher; they were beginning to disappear by now – see 6845 in 1960 for possibly the last remaining example. 'Intermediate' 3,500 gallon tender. E. Blakey, transporttreasury

Now with 4,000 gallon tender, HEWELL GRANGE is in excellent post-repair state at Gloucester Horton Road shed in March 1963. Electrification warning flashes prominent while coupled wheels have returned to the earlier pattern small bosses – compare with above. C. Leigh-Jones, ColourRail.

6840 HAZELEY GRANGE
Built September 1937

Mileages and Boilers
Date	Mileage	Boiler
From new		2973
9/3/40	86,160	2973
26/11/43	197,195	C7218
28/3/47	300,804	C2975
7/6/49	376,712	C4487
30/4/51	446,156	C4057
9/4/54	560,441	C4057
3/10/56	644,327	C8226
21/4/59	743,179	C8226
25/10/61	829,179	C2914

Sheds and Works
16/10/37	Ebbw Jct.
2/5/38	Pontypool Road
9/3/40	Wolverhampton Works **I**
3/1940	Canton
2/8/40	Shrewsbury Shops **R**
9/1940	Ebbw Jct.
14/9/40	Ebbw Jct. Shops **R**
3/5/41	Wolverhampton Works **R**
19/6/42	Pontypool Road Shops **R**
24/7/43	Pontypool Road Shops **R**
20/8/43	Pontypool Road Shops **R**
26/11/43	Swindon Works **I**
13/10/44	Reading Shops **R**
1/11/45	Pontypool Road Shops **I**
18/6/46	Westbury Shops **R**
13/8/46	Pontypool Road Shops **R**
22/11/46	Stafford Road shed **L**
28/3/47	Swindon Works **HG**
18/1/48	Ebbw Jct. **L**
15/5/48	St Philips Marsh
11/11/48	Bath Road **L**
	Tender work only
7/6/49	Swindon Works **HG**
7/10/50	Pontypool Road
30/4/51	Swindon Works **HG**
9/4/54	Swindon Works **HI**
10/11/54	Pontypool Road **U**
21/1/55	Caerphilly Works **HC**
3/10/56	Swindon Works **HG**
21/4/59	Swindon Works **HI**
7/5/60	Shrewsbury Shops **U**
15/2/61	Pontypool Road Shops **U**
23/7/61	Hereford **U**
25/10/61	Swindon Works **HG**
25/9/62	Pontypool Road **U**
22/5/63	Worcester Shops **U**
29/6/63	Neath
2/2/64	Neath Shops **U**
7/4/64	Neath Shops **U**
22/6/64	Llanelly

Tenders
Date	Tender
From new	2334
18/1/48	1899
7/6/49	1986
9/3/51	2699
30/4/51	2827
9/4/54	2246
10/11/54	2562
2/10/55	2660
3/10/56	2833
21/4/59	2340
25/10/61	2265

Mileage at 28/12/63 897,985
Withdrawn 22/2/65

A grime-coated 6840 at Bournemouth shed on 3 September 1960. L.W. Rowe, ColourRail.

6840 HAZELEY GRANGE at Shrewsbury shed early in BR days; a well-filled low-sided tender carrying (this requires the eye of faith) the GW with the coat of arms in between. Stencilled GWR SPM shed allocation still there behind buffer beam.

6841 MARLAS GRANGE
Built September 1937

Mileages and Boilers
From new		2975
13/4/40	85,871	2975
19/4/44	204,490	C2954
8/2/47	303,873	C4441
13/5/49	389,218	C8231
2/8/51	451,045	C4965
19/4/53	530,060	C4965
9/10/53	538,701	C2816
29/1/57	615,421	C8228
30/6/60	714,505	C4954
15/2/63	802,724	C6211

Sheds and Works
13/11/37	Oxley
29/4/39	Tyseley
13/4/40	Wolverhampton Works **I** Tender repaired
4/1940	Banbury
15/11/41	Bath Road Shops **R**
4/5/42	Swindon Works **R**
8/6/42	Taunton Shops **R**
17/8/42	Swindon Works **L**
10/10/42	Worcester Shops **R**
24/10/43	Banbury Shops **R**
19/4/44	Swindon Works **HG**
5/9/45	Banbury Shops **R**
1/2/46	Banbury Shops **R**
30/6/46	Banbury Shops **R**
5/9/46	Taunton Shops **R**
8/2/47	Swindon Works **I**
13/5/49	Swindon Works **HG**
17/3/50	Banbury Shops **U**
28/6/50	Banbury Shops **U**
15/7/50	Birkenhead*
2/8/51	Swindon Works **HI**
25/1/53	Birkenhead Shops **U**
15/6/53	Birkenhead Shops **U**
9/10/53	Swindon Works **HI**
17/2/56	Stafford Rd **LC**
29/1/57	Swindon Works **HG**
14/6/58	St. Philips Marsh
16/7/58	Ebbw Jct. Shops **U**
9/10/58	St. Philips Marsh Shops **U**
30/6/60	Swindon Works **HI**
24/4/61	Didcot Shops **U**
17/12/61	St. Philips Marsh Shops **U**
8/3/62	St. Philips Marsh Shops **U**
6/10/62	Southall
15/2/63	Swindon Works **HG**
29/7/64	Oxford

Birkenhead GW incorporated into LMR shed as 6C

Tenders
From new	1759
14/4/42	2888
17/8/42	2879
6/4/44	2107
8/2/47	1798
13/5/49	2251
2/8/51	2121
29/1/57	2668
30/6/60	2582
15/2/63	2817

Mileage at 28/12/63, 825,472
Withdrawn 3/6/65

MARLAS GRANGE at Southall shed on 10 October 1963 with the curious nod to decorum that appeared around this time, the white-painted smokebox door straps, which really only highlighted the almost inevitably dire state of the rest of the paintwork – though there *is* lined green under there, if you look closely. R.C. Riley, transporttreasury

Comprehensively filthy, draped in white solids left by priming, general grime and dirt topped by fine swirling ash from fire cleaning, 6841 MARLAS GRANGE stands in otherwise perfect condition at its home shed coal stage at St Philips Marsh. This would be about 1958-59, before the electrification flashes and with its previous Swindon Heavy a distant memory. One firebox plug cover missing and the other one dangling from a single bolt makes one ask why the GWR ever bothered to have these covers in the first place. No other company fitted them – they simply left the plugs uncovered in their naked glory, the locos looking the better for it. J. Davenport, Initial Photographics.

6842 NUNHOLD GRANGE
Built September 1937

Sheds and Works
16/10/37	St Philips Marsh
14/10/39	Swindon Works **I**
14/4/42	Swindon Works **I**
17/10/44	Swindon Works **HG**
21/11/44	Leamington Spa
28/12/46	Bath Road Shops
22/2/47	St. Philips Marsh
21/2/48	Swindon Works **I**
20/5/50	Swindon Works **HG**
23/3/52	Swindon Works **HG**
21/2/53	Newton Abbot Works
4/12/54	Swindon Works **HI**
9/4/57	Swindon Works **HG**
2/4/60	Swindon Works **HG**
27/1/62	Penzance
21/4/62	St. Philips Marsh
6/10/62	Stourbridge
14/11/62	Swindon Works **HI**
18/4/64	Tyseley

Tenders
From new	1702
1940	1701
1942	2881
1948	1682
1950	2213
1952	2692
1954	2246 [20/12/54]
1958	2237
1960	2895
1964	2752

NO FURTHER DETAIL

Withdrawn 11/64

6842 NUNHOLD GRANGE outside the works at Swindon in the snow. There is no date but 5079 LYSANDER in front is an indication of the period (see *The Book of the Castle 4-6-0s*). The Grange and the Castle were in for major overhauls together more than once but the only period to match the unlined black and the snow is February-March 1952. Red background to plates. J.L. Stevenson, courtesy Hamish Stevenson.

6842 at St Philips Marsh shed; this is probably 1962, after a short spell at Penzance for the broccoli traffic had taken it away from its Bristol home for the first time in years. J. Davenport, Initial Photographics.

6842 in an embarrassing conjunction with a BR Standard tender at Swindon on 19 May 1957. Actually it doesn't look all that bad... D.M. Alexander, transporttreasury

6843 POULTON GRANGE
Built October 1937

Mileages and Boilers
Date	Mileage	Boiler
From new		2977
5/4/40	86,889	2977
16/4/43	182,486	C7209
26/7/46	281,346	C3005
15/12/48	365,188	C2869
17/4/51	454,542	C7255
3/9/53	534,719	C4445
17/2/56	626,436	C2947
3/10/58	715,305	C4901
12/1/62	822,046	C4990

Sheds and Works
13/11/37	Banbury
3/5/39	Banbury Shops **R**
22/9/39	Swindon Works **L**
4/1940	Tyseley
5/4/40	Swindon Works **I**
16/9/41	Old Oak Shops **R**
16/4/43	Swindon Works **HG**
6/4/44	Tyseley Shed **R**
11/1944	Leamington Spa
23/2/45	Swindon Works **L**
6/1945	Tyseley
21/1/46	Tyseley Shed **R**
26/7/46	Swindon Works **I**
12/4/48	Wolverhampton Works **R**
15/12/48	Swindon Works **I**
20/12/49	Tyseley Shops **U**
17/4/51	Swindon Works **HI**
3/12/51	Tyseley Shops **U**
17/7/53	Tyseley Shed **U**
3/9/53	Swindon Works **HG**
16/7/55	Carmarthen
17/2/56	Swindon Works **HI**
3/11/56	Goodwick
1/12/56	Llanelly
15/4/57	Llanelly Shops **U**
2/12/57	Llanelly Shops **U**
3/11/56	Goodwick
30/10/58	Swindon Works **HG**
By 3/59	Llanelly
21/5/61	Ebbw Jct. Shops **U**
12/1/62	Swindon Works **HI**

Tenders
Date	Tender
From new	1804
5/4/40	2068
16/4/43	2894
23/2/45	1986
26/9/46	2131
9/1/48	2534
15/12/48	2219
17/4/51	2252
3/9/53	2260
17/2/56	2080
3/10/58	2260
12/1/62	2247

Mileage at 28/12/63 880,288
Withdrawn 26/2/64 Sold to Cohens, Morriston 24/4/64

Tyseley's 6843 POULTON GRANGE at what could be Neyland shed; still with early form of tapered buffers, 'intermediate' 3,500 gallon tender, plain black.

POULTON GRANGE at Old Oak Common on 18 March 1956 now with a low-sided tender. Peter Groom.

Servicing at Southall on 5 May 1956; a Carmarthen and Goodwick engine in these years, POULTON GRANGE is a long way from home. RailOnline.

6844 PENHYDD GRANGE
Built October 1937

Mileages and boilers
From new		2985
29/3/40	88,738	2985
23/3/43	185,016	C4977
30/10/45	269,587	C4977
24/9/46	291,814	C2807
5/3/48	336,184	C2807
31/8/49	383,966	C8245
13/3/51	428,163	C2949
30/10/53	515,741	C4431
20/4/56	594,333	C2914
12/11/58	684,415	C2914
16/6/61	769,657	C4054

Sheds and Works
16/10/37	Banbury
29/340	Swindon Works **I**
4/4/40	Stafford Road
31/7/42	Stafford Road Shed **R**
23/3/43	Swindon Works **HG**
21/4/44	Old Oak Shed **R**
1/12/44	Swindon Works **L**
25/4/45	Stafford Road Shed **R**
30/10/45	Swindon Works **I**
30/11/45	Newton Abbot Works **L**
17/2/46	Taunton Shops **R**
24/9/46	Swindon Works **L**
4/1/47	Tyseley Shops **R**
5/3/48	Swindon Works **I**
24/11/48	Stafford Road Shed **L**
25/1/49	Oxford Shops **U**
26/249	Birkenhead
31/8/49	Swindon Works **HC**
13/3/51	Swindon Works **HG**
8/9/51	Oxley
19/2/52	Tyseley Shops **U**
14/6/52	Llanelly
12/6/53	Llanelly Shops **U**
30/10/53	Swindon Works **HI**
30/8/55	Duffryn Yard **U**
20/4/56	Swindon Works **HG**
8/5/56	Gloucester Shops **U**
18/11/58	Caerphilly Works **HI**
16/6/61	Swindon Works **HG**
2/12/61	Neath
21/2/62	Neyland Shops **U**
11/8/62	Llanelly
18/4/63	Neath Shops **U**

Tenders
From new	2004
23/3/43	2920
1/12/44	1934
24/946	1777
5/3/48	2076
31/8/49	1974
13/3/51	2760
21/2/53	2251
30/10/53	1898
20/4/56	2824
16/6/61	2538
14/7/62	4008

Mileage at 28/12/63 835,698
Withdrawn 8/4/64 Sold to Birds, Morriston 3/6/64

With Everything Falling Apart, 6844 was notable as the Grange running latterly with a Hawksworth flat-sided tender – No.4008, see above. Here it is with the 3.17pm Oxford-Birmingham train approaching Banbury on 22 September 1962. B. Wadey, transporttreasury

6844 PENHYDD GRANGE at Cardiff Canton shed; unlined black, taper buffers, 'intermediate' tender bearing no emblem or lettering and red background to plates. That mountain of coal looks pretty close to the loading gauge....

6845 PAVILAND GRANGE
Built October 1937

Shed and Works
13/11/37	Worcester
16/9/39	Swindon Works
March 1941	Swindon Works
16/3/42	Swindon Works
18/7/44	Swindon Works 80,242 262,177
10/3/47	Swindon Works 85,309
20/7/48	Swindon Works
31/10/49	Swindon Works 74,838 160,147
By 6/50	Westbury
3/12/50	St. Philips Marsh
24/3/52	Swindon Works 85,916 85,916
30/8/54	Swindon Works **HI** 93,939
5/11/55	Hereford
31/12/55	Penzance
27/7/56	Newton Abbot Works **LC**
1/3/57	Swindon Works **HG**
31/12/58	Stafford Road Works **HI**
18/6/60	Laira
8/10/60	Oxley
17/11/62	Tyseley

Tenders
From new	2077
1942	2876
1944	2381
1948	2358
1950	2250 [4/11/49]
1952	2355
1958	2390
1962	2255 [22/12/64]

NO FURTHER DETAIL

Withdrawn 26/9/64

6845 PAVILAND GRANGE heads the Cornish Riviera out of Plymouth North Road, bound for London, 13 October 1956. It is piloting a King, nearly invisible in the shadow under the bridge. Peter Kerslake, transporttreasury

6845 PAVILAND GRANGE at Penzance shed on 9 April 1960. It still has the first emblem (not of itself a particularly remarkable survival) but it also retains the vacuum pump lubricator on the running plate by the leading splasher – this would be *the* last, you'd think and a long time after HEWELL on page 95, certainly. The distinctive horizontal row of rivets on the tender, low down, shows particularly well – the angle of the tender sides, however subtly, was different because of this, or became different over time. The difference showed up in certain light, and it often stands out as somehow separate. R.C. Riley, transporttreasury

6846 RUCKLEY GRANGE
Built October 1937

Mileages and Boilers

Date	Mileage	Boiler
From new		7231
27/9/39	93,724	7231
12/4/43	200,340	7231
21/12/45	281,566	C7235
27/8/48	366,426	C7261
1/9/50	437,187	C8209
22/10/52	517,445	C7202
25/8/55	618,366	C9208
22/11/57	696,463	C8284
16/5/60	785,823	C8265
8/2/63	883,058	C8217

Sheds and Works

13/11/37	Westbury
27/9/39	Wolverhampton Works I
9/12/39	St. Philips Marsh
31/7/41	St. Philips Marsh Shops R
4/2/42	St. Philips Marsh Shops R
1/3/42	Newton Abbot Works R
12/4/43	Swindon Works I
30/11/43	Laira Shops R
2/11/44	Bath Road Shops R
19/12/44	Swindon Works R
12/3/45	Laira Shops R
14/9/45	Old Oak Shops R
21/12/45	Swindon Works HG
21/12/46	Laira Shops R
9/9/47	Newton Abbot Shed R
8/10/47	Bath Road Shops L Tender work only
3/2/48	St. Philips Marsh Shops R
24/3/48	St. Philips Marsh Shops R
27/8/48	Swindon Works I
4/6/49	St. Philips Marsh Shops U
21/10/49	Bath Road Shops U
1/9/50	Swindon Works HG
6/4/51	Exeter Shops U
22/10/52	Swindon Works HG
3/11/54	Bath Road Shops LC
29/3/55	St. Philips Marsh Shops U
25/8/55	Swindon Works HG
3/1/56	Laira Shops U
4/9/56	Reading Shops U
22/11/57	Swindon Works HI
8/10/58	Wolverhampton Works U
16/5/60	Swindon Works HG
8/2/63	Swindon Works HI
27/2/264	Worcester Shops U
22/6/64	Barrow Road

Tenders

Date	Tender
From new	2179
29/2/42	2210
11/11/44	3014
22/11/44	2029
27/8/48	2257
1/9/50	2822
22/10/52	2786
22/11/57	1898
31/10/59	2713
16/5/60	2932
20/5/61	2928
8/2/63	2809

Mileage at 28/12/63 911,278
Withdrawn 28/9/64

6846 RUCKLEY GRANGE at Shrewsbury shed with low-sided tender in lined green, second emblem, and amused Fireman. J. Davenport, Initial Photographics.

Leaving Teignmouth in 1957. 6846 was a Bristol St Philips Marsh engine for almost its entire life, until the last year or two when steam was concentrated at the former Midland shed at Barrow Road. 527 denoted the 9.43am Paignton-Birmingham Moor Street via Swindon and Oxford – a fairly typical summer Saturday 280 mile through run. transporttreasury

6846 RUCKLEY GRANGE parked outside the modern office block, where diesel drivers were given lectures prior to taking up training on the new locos, at Old Oak Common on 3 March 1963. Peter Groom.

6847 TIDMARSH GRANGE
Built October 1937

Mileages and Boilers
Date	Mileage	Boiler
From new		7232
8/1/40	89,594	7232
4/5/43	193,931	R9222
28/10/46	290,395	C2926
15/10/48	347,338	C8269
5/4/51	434,754	C2967
24/6/53	509,228	C4059
14/7/55	600,308	C4059
16/1/58	689,742	C9220
9/12/60	782,313	C8281
5/7/63	854,550	C8225

Sheds and Works
13/11/37	Weymouth
26/6/38	St. Philips Marsh
4/8/38	St. Philips Marsh Shops **R**
2/3/39	St. Philips Marsh Shops **R**
8/1/40	Swindon Works **I**
4/1940	Tyseley
22/8/41	Tyseley Shops **R**
4/1/43	Tyseley Shed **R**
4/5/43	Swindon Works **HG**
5/10/43	Tyseley Shops **R**
2/11/43	Oxley Shops **R**
4/5/44	Newton Abbot Works **R**
10/10/44	Tyseley Shed **R**
26/5/45	Tyseley Shops **R**
17/11/45	Tyseley Shed **R**
18/3/46	Tyseley Shops **L**
9/5/46	Tyseley Shops **R**
28/10/46	Swindon Works **I**
19/947	Leamington Spa
14/6/47	Tyseley
4/10/47	Leamington Spa
1/11/47	Tyseley
24/12/47	Wolverhampton Works **L**
30/1/48	Worcester Shops **R**
15/10/48	Swindon Works **I**
27/3/50	Tyseley Shops **U**
11/9/50	Shrewsbury Shops **U**
5/4/51	Swindon Works **HI**
23/5/51	Swindon Works **U**
1/11/52	Ebbw Jct.
24/6/53	Swindon Works **HG**
14/7/55	Caerphilly Works **HI**
18/9/56	Ebbw Jct. Shops **U**
16/1/58	Swindon Works **HG**
28/11/59	Canton
12/2/60	Wolverhampton Works **LC**
27/6/60	Bath Road Shops **U**
9/12/60	Swindon Works **HG**
15/6/62	Taunton Shops **U**
1/10/62	Ebbw Jct. Shops **U**
8/9/62	Cardiff East Dock
21/2/63	Hereford Shops **U**
5/7/63	Swindon Factory **HG**
12/7//64	Gloucester Shops **U**
7/8/65	Ebbw Jct.
6/11/65	Worcester

Tenders
Date	Tender
From new	2064
28/10/46	2077
15/10/48	1816
30/12/50	2069
15/4/51	1819
19/2/52	2089
24/6/53	2355
16/1/58	1948
9/12/60	2721
5/7/63	2800

Mileage at 28/12/63, 870,784
Withdrawn 3/12/65

6847 TIDMARSH GRANGE, lined green with small tender at Newport station, 27 September 1958. Enlarged form of cover boiler/smokebox, with plate covering valve missing. Ebbw Junction had kept it well since a Heavy overhaul some months earlier. R.J. Buckley, Initial Photographics.

TIDMARSH GRANGE, now with 4,000 gallon tender, at Cardiff General with a train from Portsmouth in 1961. Norman Preedy Archive.

6848 TODDINGTON GRANGE
Built October 1937

Mileages and Boilers

Date	Mileage	Boiler
From new		7233
26/6/40	94,568	7233
27/2/43	170,486	C7236
15/10/45	262,902	C4931
28/1/47	314,077	C8252
18/5/49	395,810	C8270
6/11/51	494,677	R6201
10/5/54	579,777	C6204
28/9/56	674,976	C4977
26/6/58	761,452	C4977
2/2/61	834,424	C4977
13/2/64	903,791	C8236

Sheds and Works

13/11/37	Stafford Road
26/6/40	Wolverhampton Works **I**
3/5/41	Didcot Shops **R**
2/1/42	Stafford Road Shed **R**
2/10/42	Old Oak Shops **R**
27/2/43	Swindon Works **HG**
17/3/45	Stafford Road Shed **R**
15/10/45	Swindon Works **I**
28/1/47	Swindon Works **I**
5/4/47	Llanelly Shops **R**
14/10/48	Newton Abbot Works **R**
18/5/49	Swindon Works **HG**
6/11/51	Swindon Works **HG**
1/12/51	Oxley
1/6/52	Llanelly
27/2/54	Truro
4/3/54	Truro Shops **U**
10/5/54	Swindon Works **HI**
22/5/54	Newton Abbot
23/3/55	Taunton
31/12/55	Laira
22/3/56	Southall Shops **U**
28/9/56	Swindon Works **HG**
21/1/58	Exeter Shops **U**
29/1/58	Newton Abbot Works **U**
20/2/58	Newton Abbot Works **U**
22/3/58	Banbury
26/6/58	Wolverhampton Works **HI**
12/7/58	Laira
4/20/58	Oxford
11/3/59	Stafford Road Shed **LC**
28/11/59	Pontypool Road
2/2/61	Caerphilly Works **HG**
16/9/61	Gloucester Barnwood Shops **U**
16/2/62	Caerphilly Works **LC**
1/6/62	Pontypool Road Shops **U**
23/4/63	Ebbw Jct. Shops **U**
15/9/63	Stourbridge Shops **U**
28/11/63	Ebbw Jct. Shops Cond. 22/11/63*
27/1/64	Worcester
14/2/64	Swindon Works **HI**

*As listed on GWR History Sheet

Tenders

Date	Tender
From new	2358
27/2/43	2331
15/10/45	1719
24/11/46	2024
28/1/47	2328
18/5/49	2249
6/11/51	2247
10/5/54	2833
28/9/56	2663
14/2/64	2412

Mileage at 28/12/63, 903,791
Withdrawn 31/12/65

6848 TODDINGTON GRANGE at Birmingham Snow Hill with a stopping train for Wolverhampton Low Level, 15 May 1964. It was one of the last of the class to have a Heavy repair, in early 1964. ColourRail.

In altogether more prosaic circumstances, at Gloucester Central with a train of ballast from Tidenham Quarry, 22 October 1964; 6848 had been at Worcester for some months by now, but no one had got round to fixing the shed plate. Norman Preedy Archive.

6849 WALTON GRANGE
Built October 1937

Mileages and Boilers

10/37		7234
24/5/40	88,433	7234
26/8/43	186,110	C7207
9/5/46	273,239	C2869
13/9/48	357,618	C4924
10/1/51	434,630	C7207
11/6/53	526,829	C9219
20/10/55	619,145	C8261
19/3/58	712,249	C9218
11/4/61	833,943	C9218
28/12/63	901,049	C8232

Sheds and Works

13/11/37	Oxley
1/4/39	Banbury
24/5/40	Swindon Works **I**
27/4/42	Stourbridge Shops **R**
12/2/43	Banbury Shops **R**
26/8/43	Swindon Works **HG**
6/9/43	Swindon Works **R**
12/9/44	Banbury Shops **R**
15/4/45	Banbury Shops **R**
12/9/45	Worcester shops **R**
6/11/45	Laira Shops **R**
29/11/45	Banbury shops **R**
9/5/46	Swindon Works **I**
14/11/47	Banbury shops **R**
13/9/48	Swindon Works **I**
By 6/50	St Philips Marsh
1/6/50	Swindon Shed **LC**
4/11/50	Pontypool Road
10/1/51	Swindon Works **HI**
11/6/53	Swindon Works **HG**
9/10/54	Chester
16/7/55	Hereford
20/10/55	Swindon Works **HI**
31/12/55	Truro
11/8/56	Ebbw Jct.
11/1/57	Danygraig Shops **U**
13/7/57	Laira
9/10/57	Laira Shops **U**
19/3/58	Swindon Works **HG**
6/5/59	Westbury Shops **U**
11/7/59	Penzance
18/6/60	Laira
8/10/60	Canton
18/10/60	Canton Shops **U**
5/11/60	St. Philips Marsh
11/4/61	Caerphilly works **HI**
27/1/62	Ebbw Jct.
6/10/62	Didcot
2/11/63	Oxford
19/2/64	Swindon Works **HG**

Tenders

From new	1895
26/8/43	1748
21/8/48	1675
4/9/48	1815
13/9/48	2329
10/1/51	2259
11/9/54	2243
20/10/55	2265
4/8/56	2907
1/12/56	2911
19/3/58	1719
19/2/64	2257

Mileage at 28/12/63 901,049
Withdrawn 31/12/65

Time for a smoke while attending to 6849 WALTON GRANGE at Penzance shed; the local 83G plate indicates the period to be July 1959-June 1960; there is lined green under that grime. Note the enlarged cover above the ejector pipe. A. Robey, transporttreasury

WALTON GRANGE at Swindon shed, 1952; 'intermediate' 3,500 gallon tender. Michael Boakes Collection.

6849 WALTON GRANGE at Oxford shed, its final home, about 1964. This Grange had a unique livery history: ex-works 3/58 in lined green, ex-Caerphilly Works 4/61 in plain green, returned to lined green 2/64. J. Davenport, Initial Photographics.

6850 CLEEVE GRANGE

Built October 1937

Mileages and Boilers

Date	Mileage	Boiler
From new		7235
14/12/39	93,948	7235
12/2/43	197,924	7235
23/7/45	280,595	C2949
2/4/48	366,925	C2949
22/8/50	443,802	C4063
1/4/53	538,054	C8209
24/9/54	594,665	C2891
13/12/55	636,561	C4025
15/8/58	739,330	C4025
29/6/61	852,271	C2983
27/2/64	935,655	C4993

Sheds and Works

12/11/37	Westbury
1/4/39	St. Philips Marsh
14/12/39	Swindon Works **I**
11/11/41	St. Philips Marsh **R**
22/4/42	St. Philips Marsh **R**
12/2/43	Swindon Works **I**
20/5/44	Bath Road Shops **R**
23/7/45	Swindon Works **HG**
29/12/45	Old Oak Shops **R**
13/6/46	Newton Abbot Works **L**
17/10/46	Bath Road Shops **R**
6/12/46	Newton Abbot Shed **R**
8/4/47	Laira Shops **R**
25/6/47	St. Philips Marsh **L**
2/4//48	Swindon Works **I**
26/10/48	Bath Road Shops **R**
15/5/50	St. Philips Marsh **U**
22/8/50	Swindon Works **HG**
24/12/51	St. Philips Marsh shops **U**
1/11/52	Swindon
1/4/53	Swindon Works **HG**
24/9/54	Swindon Works **HC**
13/12/55	Swindon Works **HG**
28/12/57	Laira
15/8/58	Swindon Works **HI**
21/8/59	Newton Abbot Works **U**
31/10/59	Ebbw Jct.
29/6/61	Swindon Works **HG**
6/4/63	Pontypool Road
27/2/64	Swindon Works **HI**
22/6/64	Severn Tunnel Junction

Tenders

Date	Tender
From new	2034
14/12/39	2045
12/2/43	1728
23/7/45	2899
13/6/46	2671
8/4/47	2899
25/6/47	2443
2/4/48	1671
22/8/50	2438
1/4/53	2760
24/9/54	2574
17/8/55	2268
13/12/55	2259
19/4/56	2562
15/8/58	2587
28/11/59	2869
29/6/61	2259
27/2/64	2243

Mileage at 28/12/63 935,655
Withdrawn 14/12/64

6850 CLEEVE GRANGE, with intermediate tender, takes water while everyone's attention is on the Castle with a special; Hereford, 16 May 1964. B. Wadey, transporttreasury

Laira's 6850 CLEEVE GRANGE at Swindon shed about 1958; large tender, lined green. Norman Preedy Archive.

6851 HURST GRANGE

Built November 1937

Sheds and Works
10/12/37	Worcester
31/10/39	Swindon Works **I**
3/1940	Swindon Works
4/1941	Wolverhampton Works
4/1942	Tyseley Shops
7/1942	Worcester shops
27/11/42	Swindon Works **HG**
8/1943	Worcester Shops
9/1944	Worcester Shops
3/5/45	Swindon Works **I**
19/8/45	Swindon Works
27/11/47	Swindon Works **I**
2/10/48	Worcester Shops
27/1/50	Swindon Works **HG**
2/2/52	Swindon Works **HI**
16/2/54	Swindon Works **HG**
25/6/56	Swindon Works **HI**
15/9/58	Swindon Works **HG**
5/10/59	Wolverhampton Works **U**
13/8/60	Llanelly
8/10/60	Oxley
21/6/63	Swindon Works **HI**
19/6/65	Tyseley

Tenders
From new	1928
1940	2903
1946	1916 2121
1948	2125
1950	1875
1952	2824
1954	2251 [16/2/54]
1956	2827
1958	2268 [18/10/58]
1960	2575
1964	2912

NO FURTHER DETAIL
Withdrawn 14/8/65

6851 HURST GRANGE in the early 1950s; faded GW and coat of arms on the tender. A Worcester stalwart for years, it was one of many Granges to find itself at Oxley/Tyseley on the LMR at the end. M. Robertson, transporttreasury

Oxley's 6851 HURST GRANGE at Swindon shed on 23 June 1963, after a Heavy Intermediate at the adjacent works. A common Grange feature was the 'X' above the cabside number plate, indicating that the loco could haul loads in excess of those laid down for the class. TL. Turner, transporttreasury

6852 HEADBOURNE GRANGE

Built November 1937

Mileages and Boilers

Date	Mileage	Boiler
From new		7237
27/12/39	88,847	7237
6/7/42	167,177	7237
8/5/44	232,682	C7229
20/11/46	323,786	C9222
20/12/48	401,078	C7218
15/11/50	467,448	C2920
30/9/52	538,142	C7243
8/2/55	625,863	C4037
17/9/57	718,107	C4037
12/4/60	811,930	C2981
17/1/63	901,155	C6226

Sheds and Works

12/11/37	Weymouth
5/4/39	St. Philips Marsh Shops **R**
27/12/39	Swindon Works **I**
2/1940	St. Philips Marsh
9/12/40	St. Philips Marsh Shops **R**
9/7/41	Swindon Works **L**
6/7/42	St. Philips Marsh **I**
8/5/44	Swindon Works **HG**
6/6/45	Bath Road Shops **L**
26/11/45	St. Philips Marsh Shops **R**
20/11/46	Swindon Works **I**
16/3/48	St. Philips Marsh **L** Tender work only
20/12/48	Swindon Works **I**
15/11/50	Swindon Works **HG**
30/9/52	Swindon Works **HI**
5/2/54	St. Philips Marsh **U**
5/5/54	St. Philips Marsh **U**
8/2/55	Swindon Works **HG**
24/9/55	Bath Road Shops **U**
20/6/56	Swindon Works **LC**
8/10/56	St. Philips Marsh **U**
17/9/57	Swindon Works **HI**
8/10/58	Newton Abbot Works **LC**
12/4/60	Swindon Works **HG**
7/9/61	St. Philips Marsh Shops **U**
21/11/61	Aberdare Shops **U**
27/1/62	Ebbw Jct.
17/1/63	Swindon Works **HI**

Tenders

Date	Tender
From new	2340
9/7/41	1949
6/7/42	1904
8/5/44	2367
20/11/46	1655
20/12/48	2243
15/11/50	2907
30/9/52	2246
27/2/54	2748
17/9/57	2616
12/4/60	2866
17/1/63	2895

Mileage to 28/12/63 928,539
Withdrawn 22/1/64 Sold to J. Cashmores Newport 24/3/64

HEADBOURNE GRANGE, 4,000 gallon tender, second emblem, at Newton Abbot on 15 July 1961; the vast building behind is the Carriage & Wagon Works, with a carriage roof occupying the 'foreground'. R.C.Riley, transporttreasury

6852 HEADBOURNE GRANGE with up vans at Goring, 13 May 1955; 4,000 gallon tender, first emblem. R.C.Riley, transporttreasury

6853 MOREHAMPTON GRANGE

Built November 1937

Sheds and Works
4/3/38	Tyseley
1/4/39	Leamington Spa
27/5/39	Tyseley
6/5/40	Swindon Works **I**
11/8/43	Swindon Works **I**
5/1945	Swindon Works
8/9/45	Leamington Spa
1/12/45	Tyseley
19/8/45	Swindon Works **HG**
1/11/47	Tyseley Shops
21/2/48	Leamington Spa
22/3/48	Tyseley
12/6/48	Swindon Works
28/1/50	Swindon Works **HG**
3/2/50	Tyseley
21/7/52	Swindon Works **HI**
25/1/55	Swindon Works **HG**
21/5/57	Swindon Works **HI**
25/2/59	Swindon Works **HG**
2/11/61	Swindon Works **HI**
24/8/64	Swindon Works **HI**

Tenders
From new	2109
1940	1766
1942	2039
1946	2651 1916
1950	2716
1952	2570
1960	2258 25/2/59]
1962	2267 [2/11/61]
1964	2263 [20/8/64]

NO FURTHER DETAIL

Withdrawn 16/10/65

6853 MOREHAMPTON GRANGE northbound with a class F goods on the quadrupled section through Tyseley and Solihull where in GWR fashion the running lines were paired.

6853 MOREHAMPTON GRANGE at Swindon at an unrecorded date; this is after 1957, with the second emblem but the electrification flashes are not up, so it's probably before about 1961. I. Mackenzie, transporttreasury

6853 MOREHAMPTON GRANGE at Oxley shed, 27 August 1963. It was one of the Granges which went to its end with the 'intermediate' type of tender; note homemade front number plate. Peter Groom

6854 ROUNDHILL GRANGE
Built November 1937

Sheds and Works
10/12/37	Oxley
5/6/39	Wolverhampton Works **I**
12/7/40	Banbury
11/1941	Wolverhampton Works
29/11/43	Swindon Works **HG**
3/1945	Swindon Works
2/11/46	Swindon Works **I**
26/3/49	Swindon Works **HG**
24/4/51	Swindon Works **HI**
4/10/52	Oxley
13/6/53	Swindon Works **HG**
23/4/55	Oxford
30/9/55	Swindon Works **HG**
6/5/58	Swindon Works **HG**
By 3/59	Oxford
30/10/59	Wolverhampton Works **HC**
27/1/60	Laira
8/10/60	Canton
3/12/60	Penzance
22/4/61	Truro
7/10/61	Oxley
1/12/61	Swindon Works **HI**
19/6/65	Tyseley

Tenders
From new	1733
1944	2077
1946	1838
1948	1795
1952	2254 [2/5/51]
1956	2611
1958	2827 2252 [6/5/5/8]
1962	2402

NO FURTHER DETAIL

Withdrawn 25/9/65

6854 ROUNDHILL GRANGE at Swindon, 4 May 1958. B.K.B. Green Collection, Initial Photographics.

ROUNDHILL GRANGE ranged across the main Divisions in England and was never stationed in Wales; this is the unmistakable semi-roundhouse shed at St Blazey, the 83F Truro shed plate telling us this is 1961, when 6854 was allocated there for a few months.

In the sad 'BR Grey' but in fine fettle, ROUNDHILL GRANGE in the shed yard at Reading, 9 June 1963; front number plate gone. Peter Groom.

6855 SAIGHTON GRANGE
Built November 1937

Sheds and Works
5/3/38	Tyseley
2/7/40	Swindon Works **I**
10/1941	Swindon Works
16/11/43	Swindon Works **HG**
7/1944	Old Oak Shops
7/1945	Leamington Spa
19/8/45	Wolverhampton Works
30/11/45	Tyseley
29/12/45	Leamington Spa
23/2/46	Tyseley Shops
23/3/46	Tyseley
15/6/46	Swindon Works **I**
22/3/47	Tyseley Shops
19/4/47	Swindon Works
10/7/48	Swindon Works
10/9/49	Swindon Works **HG**
25/2/50	Laira
3/11/51	Swindon Works **HG**
27/5/54	Swindon Works **HI**
20/6/56	Swindon Works **HG**
30/5/58	Swindon Works **HI**
29/11/58	Truro
11/7/59	Penzance
28/11/59	Stourbridge
23/4/60	Tyseley
4/8/60	Swindon **HG**
6/10/62	Oxley
26/4/63	Swindon Works **HG**
17/8/63	Wolverhampton Works **U**
17/10/63	Wolverhampton Works **LC**
22/5/65	Tyseley

Tenders
From new	1780
1940	2355
1944	2179
1946	2329
1948	2265 [27/8/48]
1950	2125
1952	2932
1954	2247 [27/5/54]
1956	2251 [20/6/56]
1958	2244 [30/8/58]

NO FURTHER DETAIL

Withdrawn 25/10/65

Below. 6855 SAIGHTON GRANGE, with low-sided tender, on an up express in Hemerdon Woods, 6 August 1951. A. Lathey, transporttreasury

6855 SAIGHTON GRANGE after a heavy overhaul at Swindon; lined green, second emblem. The date is not clear, only that the work took place when the engine was at 84E Tyseley... The uncertainty is noted in the table. J. Davenport, Initial Photographics.

6856 STOWE GRANGE

Built November 1937

Mileages and Boilers
Date	Mileage	Boiler
5/8/40	94,808	7241
18/2/44	195,857	C4095
20/8/46	273,025	C8264
24/12/48	344,946	C9206
14/3/51	420,051	C7237
5/2/53	490,808	C7237
24/5/55	564,060	C8203
31/12/57	655,138	C2823
19/10/61	747,788	C8271
19/7/63	825,958	C4068

Sheds and Works
5/2/38	Stafford Road
5/8/40	Swindon Works **I**
23/8/41	Wolverhampton Works **R**
20/1/42	Wolverhampton Works **R**
16/4/42	Stafford Road Shed **R**
18/8/42	Stafford Road Shed **R**
19/1/42	Wolverhampton Works **L**
8/9/43	Stafford Road Shed **R**
18/2/44	Swindon Works **HG**
7/1945	Tyseley
12/1945	Tyseley Shops **L**
29/12/45	Stafford Road
20/8/46	Swindon Works **I**
14/12/46	Stafford Road Shed **R**
21/1/47	Wolverhampton Works **R**
1/11/47	Oxley
26/2/48	Reading Shops **L** Tender Work only
23/3/48	Oxley Shops **R**
24/12/48	Swindon Works **I**
19/5/49	Chester shops **U**
22/5/50	Oxley Shops **U**
29/6/50	Pontypool Road Shops **U**
4/8/50	Oxley Shops **U**
10/10/50	Tyseley Shops **U**
14/3/51	Swindon Works **HG**
19/4/52	Banbury
4/10/52	Oxley
5/2/53	Wolverhampton Works **HI**
13/8/53	Banbury Shops **U**
3/3/54	Oxley Shops **U**
8/10/54	Tyseley shops **U**
24/5/55	Swindon Works **HG**
3/12/55	Taunton
20/7/56	Oxley shops **U**
13/7/57	Laira
5/10/57	Worcester
31/12/57	Swindon Works **HG**
23/2/59	Hereford shops **U**
29/7/59	Gloucester Shops **U**
13/10/59	Worcester shops **U**
19/10/60	Swindon Works **HI**
15/11/61	Worcester Shops **U**
19/7/63	Swindon Works **HG**

Tenders
Date	Tender
From new	2331
2/1/42	2004
18/2/44	2887
20/8/46	1827
24/12/48	2005
5/2/53	1651
24/5/55	2756
19/10/60	2912
14/2/63	2572

Mileage at 28/12/63 838,797
Withdrawn 18/11/65

6856 STOWE GRANGE at Teignmouth in August 1957. J. Robertson, transporttreasury

STOWE GRANGE pilots 70016 ARIEL at Shrewsbury; now a Worcester engine after its few months at Laira, it stayed at 85A until withdrawn at the end of 1965. ColourRail.

6857 TUDOR GRANGE

Built November 1937

Sheds and Works

9/12/37	Landore
2/4/38	Tyseley Shops
14/10/39	Swindon Works
20/5/40	Swindon Works **I**
1/1942	Swindon Works
3/1942	Swindon Works
11/3/43	Swindon Works **I**
6/1943	Carmarthen Shops
12/3/45	Swindon Works **HG**
12/7/47	Swindon Works **I**
12/6/48	Stourbridge
31/1/49	Swindon Works **HC**
17/8/50	Swindon Works **HG**
19/4/52	Swindon Works **HC**
3/10/53	Swindon Works **HG**
10/9/55	Chester
19/5/56	Stourbridge
22/5/56	Swindon Works **HG**
5/7/56	Wolverhampton Works **LC**
5/10/57	Oxley
3/4/58	Tyseley Shops **U**
5/6/58	Wolverhampton Works **U**
18/11/58	Swindon Works **HI**
11/11/59	Old Oak Shops **U**
9/12/60	Swindon works **HG**
16/8/63	Swindon Works **HI**
22/5/65	Tyseley

Tenders

From new	1766
1940	2109
1942	1986
1944	1801
1946	2922
1948	2010
1950	2859
1952	2256 [9/5/52]
	2254 [14/10/53]
1958	2246 [18/11/58]
1960	2241
1962	2248 [1/2/61]

NO FURTHER DETAIL

Withdrawn 7/10/65

6857 TUDOR GRANGE under repair at Worcester shops, leading coupled wheels removed. Tyseley's 6857 had come in on 14 December 1953 with the right leading axle box hot, an uncommon fault on Granges. The scored axle journal was set for turning in the wheel lathe whereupon the axle was found to be bent! The wheelset had to be sent to Swindon for axle replacement. Brian Penney.

TUDOR GRANGE at Weymouth station, 7 September 1963. ColourRail.

6858 WOOLSTON GRANGE
Built December 1937

Sheds and Works
5/3/38	Tyseley
3/5/40	Wolverhampton Works **I**
9/1941	Banbury
10/1941	Tyseley
26/1/42	Swindon Works
4/9/43	Swindon Works **I**
4/1944	Swindon Works
17/5/46	Tyseley Shops
5/10/46	Swindon Works **HG**
1/11/47	Wolverhampton Works
26/2/49	Swindon Works **HG**
117/7/51	Swindon Works **HG**
12/2/54	Wolverhampton Works **HI**
11/9/54	Shrewsbury
20/5/55	Swindon Works **HC**
15/6/55	Swindon Works **X/S**
16/7/55	Landore
13/8/55	Llanelly
31/12/55	Laira
29/2/56	Newton Abbot Works **U**
13/8/56	Swindon Works **HI**
4/10/58	Oxford
19/12/58	Swindon Works **HG**
27/1/60	Penzance
23/4/60	Canton
21/5/60	Shrewsbury
16/7/60	Tyseley
6/10/62	Oxley
13/12/63	Swindon Works **HG**
19/6/65	Tyseley

Tenders
From new	2038
1944	2875
1946	1863
1948	1663
1950	1839
1952	2263 [23/8/51]
1956	2907 2827
1958	1739
1962	2262 [1/11/61]
1964	2266

NO FURTHER DETAIL

Withdrawn 9/10/65

WOOLSTON GRANGE as one of the Oxley complement, 8 August 1963, a date to remember – see 6833 for instance. J.L. Stevenson, courtesy Hamish Stevenson.

Tyseley's 6858 WOOLSTON GRANGE at Swindon shed, about 1961. It has a low-sided tender, 1739 attached in 1958.

6859 YIEWSLEY GRANGE

Built December 1937

Mileages and boilers

Date	Mileage	Boiler
2/37		7244
19/3/40	91,375	7244
30/10/42	193,900	C2838
15/5/46	275,962	C2838
12/12/47	312,078	C2951
23/3/50	366,531	C4917
24/6/52	433,056	C2826
25/2/53	465,131	C2860
19/4/53	470,522	C2860
28/1/55	512,378	C8274
17/1/58	581,165	C8274
23/12/60	690,460	C8238
13/2/64	779,297	C7205

Sheds and Works

8/1/38	St. Philips Marsh
27/1/39	St. Philips Marsh shops **R**
19/3/40	Swindon Works **I**
6/6/40	Swindon Works **L**
7/1940	Chester
27/12/40	Swindon Works **L**
30/10/42	Swindon Works **I**
13/10/43	Swindon Works **L**
20/4/44	Chester Shops **R**
25/9/45	Chester Shops **R**
23/10/45	Swindon shed **R**
16/2/46	Stourbridge Shops **R**
15/5/46	Stafford Road Works **I**
20/7/46	Chester Shops **R**
4/9/46	Chester Shops **R**
1/8/47	Chester Shops **R**
12/12/47	Stafford Road Works **L**
20/5/48	Chester Shops **R**
26/2/49	Birkenhead*
3/6/49	Birkenhead Shops **U**
3/11/49	Tyseley Shops **U**
7/11/49	Tyseley Shed **U**
22/12/49	Tyseley Shops **U**
31/1/50	Laira Shops **U**
23/3/50	Swindon Works **HG**
24/3/52	Swindon Works **U**
24/6/52	Swindon Works **HI**
25/2/53	Swindon Works **HC**
28/1/55	Swindon Works **HG**
2/9/55	St. Philips Marsh shops **U**
26/10/56	Oxley Shops **U**
17/1/58	Swindon Works **HI**
14/6/58	St. Philips Marsh

*Birkenhead GW incorporated into LMR shed as 6C

21/2/59	Newton Abbot
24/2/59	Newton Abbot Works **U**
16/5/59	Oxford
8/8/59	Canton
30/5/60	Canton Shops **U**
13/12/60	Swindon Works **HG**
25/8/61	Aberdare Shops **U**
20/9/61	Aberdare Shops **U**
8/9/62	Cardiff East Dock
28/2/63	Caerphilly Works **LC**
13/2/64	Swindon Works **HG**
7/8/65	Severn Tunnel Jct.

Tenders

Date	Tender
From new	2368
19/3/40	1804
30/10/42	1844
30/10/48	2251
26/3/49	2010
5/11/49	2382*

*Early Collett tender, one of ten numbered 2373-2383; generally as Churchward but with longer fender and slightly higher sides.

Date	Tender
23/3/50	2113
24/6/52	2551
17/1/58	2778
23/12/60	4018
13/2/64	2259

Mileage to 28/12/63 779,297
Withdrawn 18/11/65

6859 YIEWSLEY GRANGE with a decent look at the rear of a tender for once; Birkenhead shed, c.1957. J. Davenport, Initial Photographics.

6859 YIEWSLEY GRANGE at Ruabon, 5 July 1952. 6859 was involved in a firebox failure on 22 December 1952, while at Wrexham on a goods from Birkenhead to London. The crown collapsed due to a false water gauge reading and the Fireman was seriously injured. Both the signalman and nearby residents heard the explosion. As is often the case, a series of minor human failures, none of them conclusive by itself, had contributed to the incident, beginning with a misalignment of the gauge glass in its frame. Ray Hinton Archive, courtesy Norman Preedy.

YIEWSLEY GRANGE with an up freight, running into Birmingham Snow Hill on 26 February 1958. It carries the shed plate 6C, the WR shed at Birkenhead having been subsumed into the LMR scheme of things, at least officially. Michael Mensing.

6860 ABERPORTH GRANGE
Built February 1939

Mileages and Boilers
From new		4061
4/4/42	99,619	4061
1/1/43	123,891	C4091
4/1/45	188,267	C4472
16/11/46	261,795	C7209
19/5/49	336,807	C2837
4/3/52	422,625	C4441
24/9/54	515,639	C2901
18/1/57	616,543	C2901
25/6/59	724,862	C8207
31/8/62	812,264	C7221

Sheds and Works
1/4/39	Tyseley
6/3/41	Tyseley Shops **R**
26/3/41	Bristol Shops **R**
20/12/41	Tyseley Shops **R**
4/4/42	Swindon Works **I**
1/1/43	Swindon Works **L**
15/10/43	Tyseley Shed **R**
4/1/45	Swindon Works **I**
6/10/45	Leamington Spa
1/12/45	Tyseley
18/2/46	Worcester Shops **R**
6/5/46	Bath Road Shops **R**
16/11/46	Swindon Works **HG**
21/1/47	Wolverhampton Works **R**
29/4/48	Old Oak Common Shops **R**
10/9/48	Tyseley Shops **L**
21/1/49	Taunton Shops **U**
26/2/49	Birkenhead
19/5/49	Swindon Works **HG**
24/11/50	Swindon Works **LC**
6/10/51	Oxley
4/3/52	Swindon Works **HI**
1/11/52	Banbury
21/12/52	Banbury Shops **U**
11/7/53	Laira
3/10/53	Pontypool Road
26/12/53	Penzance
24/9/54	Swindon Works **HG**
13/8/55	Newton Abbot
10/9/55	Hereford
3/12/55	Penzance
18/1/57	Swindon Works **HI**
25/6/59	Swindon Works **HG**
8/10/60	Llanelly
3/12/60	Taunton
17/6/61	Laira
19/5/62	St. Philips Marsh
31/8/62	Swindon Works **HI**
9/5/63	Wolverhampton Works **LC**
22/6/64	Barrow Road
5/10/64	Llanelly
7/11/64	Cardiff East Dock

Tenders
From new	1844
4/4/42	2887
1/4/45	2905
16/11/46	2367
19/5/49	1798
24/11/50	2824
4/3/52	2264
225/659	2603
31/8/62	2569

Mileage at 28/12/63 846,965
Withdrawn 8/2/65

ABERPORTH GRANGE at Worcester shed, half a year from withdrawal, on 26 July 1964. Valves are out either side with the plating removed and the valve setter has made chalk notes on the cylinder cover in the traditional way. What it took to distort the boiler hand rail like that is hard to imagine. D. Birt, transporttreasury

6860 ABERPORTH GRANGE at Penzance station, 23 July 1957. J. Davenport, Initial Photographics.

6861 CRYNANT GRANGE

Built February 1939

Sheds and Works

1/4/39	St Philips Marsh
2/8/41	Swindon Works **I**
12/1943	Swindon Works
17/5/46	Swindon Works **HG**
24/2/48	Newton Abbot Works
21/5/49	Swindon Works **HG**
4/11/50	Pontypool Road
1/12/51	Swindon Works **HI**
18/4/53	Oxley
15/6/54	Swindon Works **HI**
25/1/56	Swindon Works **HG**
24/4/58	Wolverhampton Works **U**
3/12/55	Tyseley
26/5/58	Swindon Works **HI**
31/3/60	Tyseley Shops **U**
18/12/63	Swindon Works **HG**

Tenders

From new	2005
1940	2015
1942	1983
1944	1733
1950	2064
1952	2445
1958	2638
1962	1761

NO FURTHER DETAIL

Withdrawn 16/10/65

CRYNANT GRANGE coming into Birmingham Snow Hill with a train from Bournemouth, classic work for a Grange, in August 1962. Norman Preedy Archive.

CRYNANT GRANGE coming into Birmingham Snow Hill with a train from Bournemouth, classic work for a Grange, in August 1962. Norman Preedy Archive.

6862 DERWENT GRANGE

Built February 1939

Sheds and Works
1/4/39	Oxley
29/4/39	Leamington Spa
1/1940	Swindon Works
21/4/42	Swindon Works **I**
11/1942	Swindon Works
2/1944	Swindon Works
29/12/45	Wolverhampton Works **I**
24/1/48	Swindon Works **HG**
25/3/50	Swindon Works **HG**
23/3/52	Swindon Works **HI**
28/11/53	Swindon Works **HG**
26/3/55	Oxford
23/455	Oxley
6/1/56	Swindon Works **HI**
17/4/58	Swindon Works **HG**
28/11/59	Oxley Shops **U**
5/11/62	Swindon Works **HI**
4/10/64	Swindon Works **HC**
22/5/65	Tyseley

Tenders
From new	1947
1940	1968
1944	1876
1948	1797
1950	2258 [28/4/50]
1956	2252 [6/1/56]
1958	2827
1962	2860

NO FURTHER DETAIL

Withdrawn 19/6/65

6862 DERWENT GRANGE at Kidderminster with a train from Birmingham, 5 May 1965. ColourRail.

6862 DERWENT GRANGE in the rain; large tender, second emblem, loose boiler cladding at top. transporttreasury

6863 DOLHYWEL GRANGE
Built February 1939

Mileages and Boilers
From new		4065
2/3/42	103,473	4065
3/8/44	192,101	C4989
1/11/46	269,079	C9219
28/7/49	356,487	C2887
24/1/52	443,359	C4422
31/8/54	542,149	C4422
15/3/57	628,613	C2868
19/3/59	710,734	C2868
24/1/62	810,305	C2993

Sheds and Works
1/4/39	Old Oak
29/4/39	Swindon
22/7/39	Weymouth
11/11/39	Swindon
2/3/42	Swindon Works **I**
3/1942	St. Philips Marsh
4/4/43	St. Philips Marsh Shops **R**
3/8/44	Swindon Works **HG**
1/11/46	Swindon Works **I**
26/6/47	Bath Road Shops **L**
1/4/48	St. Philips Marsh **L**
11/5/48	Swindon Works **R**
17/9/48	Wolverhampton Works **R**
20/12/48	Bath Road Shops **R**
27/5/49	Shrewsbury Shops **U**
28/7/49	Swindon Works **HG**
19/6/50	Westbury Shops **U**
21/8/51	Weymouth Shops **U**
24/1/52	Swindon Works **HG**
4/4/52	Swindon Works **U**
31/7/53	St. Philips Marsh **U**
26/5/54	Exeter Shops **U**
31/8/54	Swindon Works **HI**
29/9/56	Bath Road Shops **U**
24/12/56	Llanelly Shops **U**
15/3/57	Swindon Works **HG**
19/4/58	Oxley
14/6/58	Laira
19/3/59	Wolverhampton Works **HI**
17/5/60	Laira Shops **U**
20/10/60	Laira Shops **U**
30/12/60	Laira Shops **U**
23/2/61	Laira Shops **U**
24/1/62	Swindon Works **HI**
6/10/62	Reading
4/564	Cardiff East Dock

Tenders
From new	1661
2/3/42	2874
3/8/44	2241
12/10/46	2224
1/11/46	2064
11/5/48	2091
24/1/52	2414
4/4/52	2535
19/9/53	4037 (Hawksworth)
31/8/54	2860
3/9/56	2670
5/9/56	2594
2/10/56	2860
15/3/57	2815
31/10/59	2256
24/1/62	2816

Mileage at 28/12/63 866,376
Withdrawn 13/11/64

6863 DOLHYWEL GRANGE, new at Swindon shed in February 1939; plain green, roundel.

6863 DOLHYWEL GRANGE with lot of work under its belt, and a lot of resultant grime, at Exeter St David's on 6 August 1955, heading the 10.27am SO Cardiff-Paignton. W. Hermiston, transporttreasury

6864 DYMOCK GRANGE
Built February 1939

Sheds and Works
1/4/39	Old Oak Common
8/1941	Swindon Works **I**
2/1943	Tyseley Shops
10/2/44	Swindon Works **I**
2/1945	Reading
13/7/46	Swindon Works **HG**
29/1/49	Swindon Works **I**
2/12/50	Swindon Works **HG**
1/7/53	Swindon Works **HG**
27/2/55	Oxley
26/3/55	Oxford
13/2/56	Swindon Works **HI**
17/6/58	Swindon Works **HG**
30/10/58	Caerphilly Works **LC**
8/8/59	Canton
6/11/59	Gloucester Barnwood **U**
14/1/60	Reading Shops **U**
24/2/62	Penzance
21/4/62	St. Philips Marsh
19/5/62	Oxley
22/5/65	Tyseley
27/11/63	Swindon Works **HG**

Tenders
From new	2026
1942	2837
1944	2879
1946	2179
1950	2253 [19/12/50]
1952	2542
1962	2401

NO FURTHER DETAIL

Withdrawn 9/10/65

Looking dreadful at Oxley, weeks from withdrawal, 6 July 1965. J.L. Stevenson, courtesy Hamish Stevenson.

6864 DYMOCK GRANGE at Reading in 1949; tall chimney with capuchon, GWR on low-sided tender, the odd little vacuum pump lubricator on running plate by leading splasher, looking like someone's forgotten thermos flask and original tapered buffers. Canon Alec George, transporttreasury

A good-looking DYMOCK GRANGE, better looking at any rate than most of its contemporaries, at Old Oak Common, on 17 April 1962. That horizontal row of rivets on the tender, about 18 inches above the running plate made for small changes in the angle this lower part presented to the light, so it often stands out as somehow separate. There was some subtle distortion too, it seems, or at least the appearance of it – observe 6845 at Penzance in 1960 for instance. Peter Groom.

A closer view of 6864 at old Oak on 17 April 1962. In this period it moved from Penzance to St Philips Marsh, which perhaps explains the absence of a shed plate. Peter Groom.

6865 HOPTON GRANGE

Built March 1939

Mileages and Boilers
3/39		4051
30/4/42	106,457	4051
7/7/44	179,066	4051
30/7/46	252,082	C8258
25/1/49	354,289	C2829
5/10/51	440,410	R6200
20/8/54	533,064	R6200
19/2/57	623,787	C7213
2/11/59	723,969	C4026
8/5/62	813,876	C4026

Sheds and works
1/4/39	Old Oak
1/1941	Swindon Works
21/3/42	Swindon Works **I**
9/1943	Wolverhampton Works
23/5/44	Swindon Works **I**
14/6/46	Swindon Works **HG**
29/1/49	Swindon Works **HG**
13/8/49	Reading
17/6/50	Swindon Works
5/9/51	Swindon Works **HG**
19/6/54	Wolverhampton Works **HI**
16/7/55	Carmarthen
5/11/55	Gloucester
31/12/55	Laira
6/10/56	Ebbw Jct.
19/2/57	Swindon Works **HG**
2/11/59	Swindon Works **HI**
28/11/59	St. Philips Marsh

Tenders
From new	1902
30/4/42	2109
9/10/43	2043
7/7/44	2130
30/7/46	1986
20/3/46	1759
25/1/49	2038
24/3/44	2316
10/9/49	1931
28/7/50	2901
20/8/54	2548
8/10/54	2787
19/2/57	2612
22/2/58	2400
2/11/59	2250

Withdrawn 8/5/62, cut up 22/6/62

6865 HOPTON GRANGE new in 1939; plain green. R.C. Riley, transporttreasury

HOPTON GRANGE much later; lined green, 'intermediate' 3,500 gallon tender, vacuum pump lubricator by forward splasher long gone. In the mid-1950s this Grange was used for platform clearance tests at Clapham Junction. R.C. Riley, transporttreasury

6866 MORFA GRANGE
Built March 1939

Sheds and Works
1/4/39	Tyseley
7/2/42	Swindon Works **I**
10/1942	Swindon Works
4/1944	Leamington Spa
6/1944	Tyseley
23/9/44	Swindon Works **I**
6/1945	Tyseley shops
23/2/46	Swindon Works
15/6/46	Tyseley Shops
27/12/47	Swindon Works **HG**
28/1/50	Wolverhampton Works **HI**
14/7/51	Wolverhampton Works
30/5/52	Swindon Works **HG**
19/1/55	Swindon Works **HI**
27/6/57	Swindon Works **HG**
3/11/59	Tyseley Shops **U**
4/3/60	Swindon Works **HI**
3/12/63	Swindon Works **HG**

Tenders
From new	2227
1942	2901
1944	2921
1948	2069
1950	1886
1952	1878 2616
1956	2760
1960	2253 [4/3/60]

NO FURTHER DETAIL

Withdrawn 27/5/65

MORFA GRANGE at Reading about 1962-63. The boiler hand rail has experienced one of those mysterious 'bashes' usually ascribed (rightly or wrongly) to a fire iron carelessly lent against the loco by a shed man, doubtless wilting in the heat and dust. In this case the hand rail knob has fallen out and hangs down loose – so when modelling the 1960s anything is possible! RailOnline.

6866 MORFA GRANGE, of now-LMR shed 2A Tyseley, at Old Oak on 31 August 1964. 'Intermediate' 3,500 gallon tender. It had been one of the Granges to get a 4,000 gallon tender in the war but by 1948 had reverted for a while to the earlier low-sided type, the only one known to be lettered BRITISH RAILWAYS. Peter Groom.

6867 PETERSTON GRANGE
Built March 1939

Mileages and Boilers
From new		4053
18/2/42	105,574	4053
11/3/44	181,335	4053
11/9/45	235,210	C9219
26/6/46	262,617	C8289
30/6/48	334,704	C4448
2/10/50	425,327	C2926
10/6/52	482,581	C4966
4/11/53	535,884	C8250
13/3/56	624,395	C8258
15/10/58	718,415	C9241
28/9/61	816,184	C9241

Sheds and Works
1/4/39	St. Philips Marsh
18/2/42	Swindon Works **I**
5/4/42	St. Philips Marsh Shops **R**
11/3/44	Swindon Works **I**
11/9/45	Swindon Works **L**
29/3/46	Weymouth Shops **R**
26/6/46	Swindon Works **I**
30/6/48	Swindon Works **HG**
8/11/48	Bath Road Shops **L**
	Tender Work only
2/10/50	Swindon Works **HG**
3/11/51	Weymouth
1/12/51	St. Philips Marsh
10/6/52	Swindon Works **HC**
4/11/53	Swindon Works **HG**
27/3/54	Bath Road
19/6/54	St Philip's Marsh
13/3/56	Swindon Works **HG**
22/4/57	Laira Shops **U**
28/12/57	Laira
22/3/58	Stafford Road
17/5/58	Pontypool Road
15/10/58	Swindon Works **HG**
25/8/60	Hereford Shops **U**
18/2/61	Pontypool Road Shops **U**
28/9/61	Caerphilly Works **HI**
18/1/63	Pontypool Road Shops **U**
26/2/63	Ebbw Jct. Shops **U**
29/6/63	Neath
11/9/63	Neath Shops **U**
17/2/64	Hereford Shops **U**
22/6/64	Llanelly

Tenders
From new	2006
18/2/42	2872
11/9/45	2900
26/6/46	2358
30/6/48	2064
6/5/49	2003
2/10/50	2249
10/6/52	2367
25/7/53	1838
13/3/56	2263
15/6/58	2614
7/1961	2783

Mileage at 28/12/63 880,168
Withdrawn 10/8/64

6867 PETERSTON GRANGE, with 'intermediate' tender, on a down goods at Teignmouth, 19 July 1956. R.C. Riley, transporttreasury

Pontypool Road's tired-looking 6867 PETERSTON GRANGE at Stourbridge shed 4 May 1963; smokebox char shovel on running plate, broken 86G shed plate, cover plate on the lower boiler missing over rocker shaft. Norman Preedy Archive.

6868 PENRHOS GRANGE
Built March 1939

Mileages and Boilers
From new		4054
29/11/41	100,827	4054
12/9/44	193,424	4054
12/4/47	274,984	C2947
10/6/49	354,260	C2930
5/12/51	456,517	C8260
9/11/53	530,671	C7229
10/2/56	624,410	C4069
13/2/58	709,827	C4444
19/1/61	788,565	C4444
4/10/63	843,599	C7276

Sheds and Works
1/4/39	Ebbw Jct.
29/11/41	Swindon Works **I**
19/8/43	Ebbw Jct. Shops **R**
12/9/44	Swindon Works **I**
31/10/45	Ebbw Jct. Shed **R**
29/3/46	Banbury Shops **R**
28/1/47	Newton Abbot Works **R**
12/4/47	Swindon Works **HG**
30/6/47	Ebbw Jct, Shed **R**
11/3/48	Ebbw Jct, Shops **L**
	Tender Work only
12/6/48	Taunton
10/12/48	Taunton Shops **R**
9/2/49	Newton Abbot Works **LC**
	Tender Work only
10/6/49	Swindon Works **HG**
18/8/50	Newton Abbot Works **U**
23/5/51	Taunton Shops **U**
3/9/51	Taunton Shops **U**
6/11/51	Taunton Shops **U**
5/12/51	Swindon Works **HI**
23/4/52	Tyseley Shops **U**
8/7/53	Taunton Shops **U**
9/11/53	Swindon Works **HG**
5/11/54	Taunton Shops **U**
10/2/56	Swindon Works **HI**
13/2/58	Swindon Works **HG**
7/9/59	Exeter Shops **U**
19/2/60	Taunton Shops **U**
5/11/60	Exeter
19/1/61	Wolverhampton Works **HI**
25/2/61	Penzance
14/7/62	Laira
22/8/62	Laira Shops **U**
6/10/62	Didcot
4/10/63	Swindon Works **HG**
2/11/63	Oxford

Tenders
From new	1682
12/9/44	2892
12/6/48	2164
5/12/51	2267
9/11/53	2242
10/2/56	2262
13/2/58	2551
4/10/63	2245

Mileage at 28/12/63 849,093
Withdrawn 11/10/65

Taunton's 6868 PENRHOS GRANGE with valve setting notes still chalked on the cylinder covers, Bristol Temple Meads 12 August 1957; 'intermediate' tender, first emblem. J. Robertson, transporttreasury

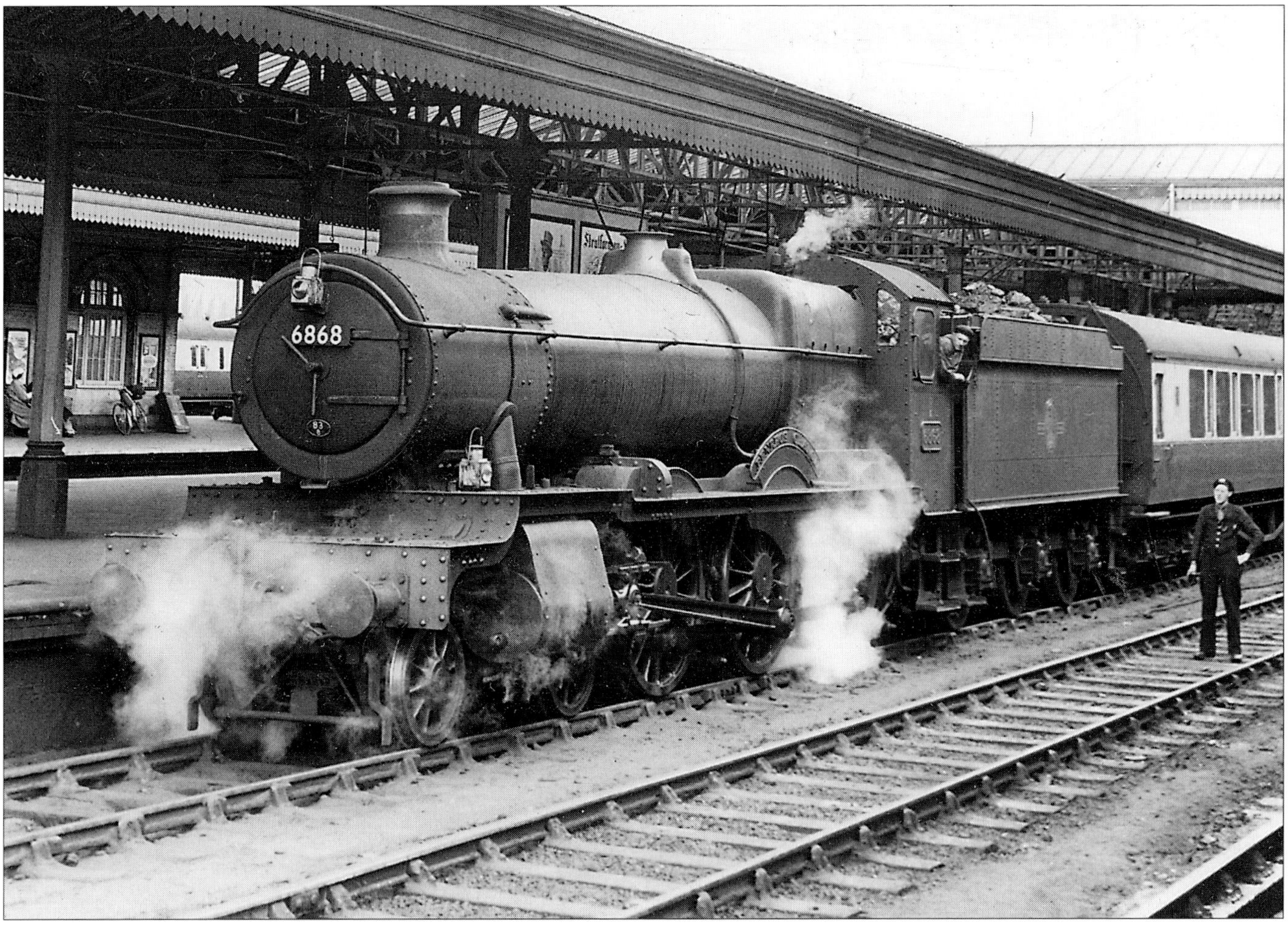

Now with 4,000 gallon tender and lined in green, at Exeter St David's, 1959. J. Davenport, Initial Photographics.

6868 PENRHOS GRANGE at Oxford station (it went to Oxford in late 1963) on 12 May 1965, only a few months before withdrawal; it has now re-acquired an 'intermediate' 3,500 gallon tender. By now Oxford was one of the last places where it was possible to see Granges (nameless like this one of course) in any number. J.L. Stevenson, courtesy Hamish Stevenson.

6869 RESOLVEN GRANGE

Built March 1939

Mileages and boilers
From new		4055
27/2/42	101,107	4055
29/6/44	176,543	4055
20/2/47	263,089	C4044
7/2/49	346,990	C3009
22/6/51	440,362	C7206
1/7/53	529,679	C2918
28/4/55	620,501	C2918
2/7/57	719,905	C4422
27/11/59	811,665	C2847
18/10/62	906,939	C6204

Sheds and Works
1/4/39	Ebbw Jct.
10/1/41	Taunton Shops **R**
27/2/42	Swindon Works **HI**
3/1942	Pontypool Road
27/3/42	Swindon Works **R**
18/10/42	Swindon Works **L**
3/1943	Old Oak
29/10/43	Old Oak Shops **L**
13/10/45	Exeter Shops **R**
9/3/46	Old Oak Shed **L**
19/8/46	Didcot Shops **R**
20/2/47	Swindon Works **HG**
11/11/48	Old Oak Shops **L**
7/2/49	Swindon Works **HI**
13/8/49	Southall
3/12/49	Penzance
30/10/50	Newton Abbot Works **LC**
17/4/51	Penzance Shops **U**
22/6/51	Swindon Works **HI**
1/7/53	Swindon Works **HG**
7/10/53	Laira Shops **U**
28/4/55	Swindon Works **HI**
28/6/56	Exeter Shops **U**
8/9/56	St. Philips Marsh
2/7/57	Swindon Works **HG**
27/11/59	Swindon Works **HI**
26/12/59	Goodwick
30/1/60	Penzance
9/3/61	Laira Shops **U**
25/1/62	Laira Shops **U**
21/4/62	St. Philips Marsh
18/10/62	Swindon Works **HG**
6/10/62	Southall
14/12/63	Reading Shops **U**
29/7/64	Cardiff East Dock

Tenders
From new	2059
27/2/42	2873
27/3/42	1844
18/10/42	2875
29/6/44	2043
20/2/47	1837
7/2/49	2254
22/4/50	2263
22/6/51	2261
1/7/53	2227
14/7/56	2638
2/7/57	2266
27/11/59	2395
18/10/62	2791

Mileage at 28/12/63 940,822
Withdrawn 21/7/65

Penzance's 6869 RESOLVEN GRANGE with the down Cornish Riviera near Devonport, 21 April 1954; black, low-sided tender. Alan Lathey, transporttreasury

RESOLVEN GRANGE pilots 1004 COUNTY OF SOMERSET at Aller Junction, August 1955. J. Robertson, transporttreasury

Good looks long gone, at Banbury (6990 alongside) on 13 March 1965. J.L. Stevenson, courtesy Hamish Stevenson.

6870 BODICOTE GRANGE
Built March 1939

Sheds and Works
29/4/39	Westbury
11/11/39	Severn Tunnel Jct.
10/1940	Severn Tunnel Jct. Shops
29/4/41	Swindon Works **I**
7/1943	Newton Abbot Works
10/1943	Severn Tunnel Jct. Shops
1/3/44	Swindon Works **HG**
3/1945	Swindon Works
29/7/46	Swindon Works **I**
2/11/46	Ebbw Jct.
3/6/49	Swindon Works **HG**
7/10/50	Swindon Works
1/12/51	Swindon Works **HG**
20/8/54	Swindon Works **HI**
16/6/56	Exeter
1/12/56	St. Philips Marsh
13/12/56	Penzance
18/6/57	Swindon Works **HG**
30/1/60	Truro
25/8/60	Swindon Works **HI**
7/10/61	Oxley
11/3/63	Swindon Works **HI**

Tenders
From new	2008
1946	1954
1950	2259 [1/7/49]
1952	2818 2743
1956	2664
1960	2735

NO FURTHER DETAIL

Withdrawn 11/9/65

A poor neglected 6870 with just its smokebox plate remaining to identify it, on a freight near Kidderminster, July 1965. ColourRail.

6870 BODICOTE GRANGE uplifted by the breakdown crane, an undated picture at an unrecorded Motive Power Depot. It is difficult to be sure with these highly standardised Churchward 'turntable units' but Oxley would be a good guess, about 1961. Both Granges, BODICOTE and the far one, 6845 PAVILAND GRANGE were there by that year, the structural and layout features match (it's not Tyseley – there would be the 'factory' on the right) and the chief shed of the District, Stafford Road, had a Ransomes Rapier crane, just like this. QED? transporttreasury

6871 BOURTON GRANGE
Built March 1939

Sheds and Works

29/4/39	Weymouth
22/739	Swindon
11/11/39	Severn Tunnel Jct.
1/1941	Swindon Works
26/5/42	Swindon Works **I**
15/8/44	Swindon Works **HG**
19/4/47	Swindon Works
15/5/48	Swindon Works I
2/12/50	Swindon Works **HG**
6/10/51	Pontypool Road
5/9/53	Swindon Works **HG**
17/11/55	Swindon Works **HI**
23/9/55	Swindon Works **HG**
1/12/56	Truro
14/6/58	Laira
13/8/58	Swindon Works **HG**
2/712/58	Penzance
21/1/59	Laira
28/11/59	Tyseley
30/1/60	Taunton
5/2/60	Newton Abbot Works **U**
13/8/60	Llanelly
13/9/60	Oxley
22/6/61	Swindon Works **HI**
18/4/63	Wolverhampton Works **U**

Tenders

From new	1850
1942	2892
1944	1988
1946	1952
1948	1748
1950	2363
1952	2243[6/12/50]
1956	2259 [11/9/54]
1958	2263[[2/10/58]

NO FURTHER DETAIL

Withdrawn 16/10/65

A splendid – for the period at least – 6871 BOURTON GRANGE, now wearing Oxley's new LMR code 2B at Basingstoke, 18 July 1964. J.A.C. Kirke, transporttreasury

At home at 2B Oxley at about the same period. Michael Boakes Collection.

That it should come to this? 6871 may look like it is being scrapped but it is actually under repair, at Banbury shed on 12 May 1965. J.L. Stevenson, courtesy Hamish Stevenson.

To prove it, here is the old girl working at Oxford on 6 July 1965. BOURTON GRANGE was finally withdrawn in October. J.L. Stevenson, courtesy Hamish Stevenson.

6872 CRAWLEY GRANGE
Built March 1939

Mileages and Boilers

From new		7262
2/4/42	100,223	7262
14/3/45	201,924	C2845
30/10/47	290,777	C4479
12/9/50	401,851	C2863
19/5/52	453,838	C8217
4/12/53	511,076	C7212
23/11/55	586,674	C7212
6/6/58	670,390	C2939
21/4/61	761,283	C4942
15/11/63	831,892	C8211

Sheds and Works

29/4/39	Weymouth
9/12/39	Severn Tunnel Jct.
16/11/40	Severn Tunnel Jct. Shops **R**
15/11/41	Severn Tunnel Jct. Shops **R**
2/4/42	Swindon Works **I**
4/4/42	Laira
16/11/43	Newton Abbot Works **L**
30/11/43	Laira Shops **R**
4/3/44	Reading Shops **R**
22/3/44	Laira Shops **R**
2/1/45	Laira Shops **R**
14/3/45	Swindon Works **HG**
29/6/45	St, Blazey Shops **L**
26/10/45	Laira Shops **R**
13/3/46	Laira Shops **R**
16/8/46	St. Blazey Shops **L**
19/1/47	Laira Shops R
22/2/47	Landore
30/10/47	Swindon Works **I**
2/10/48	Truro
4/11/48	Laira Shops **R**
22/3/49	Laira Shops **R**
19/7/49	Newton Abbot Works **LC**
1/11/49	Truro Shops **U**
5/5/50	Truro shops **U**
26/7/50	Truro Shops **U**
12/9/50	Swindon Works **HG**
2/12/50	Severn Tunnel Jct.
24/3/51	Pontypool Road
21/7/51	Gloucester Shops **U**
19/7/52	Swindon Works **HC**
4/12/53	Swindon Works **HG**
23/11/55	Swindon Works **HI**
9/7/56	Pontypool Road Shops **U**
11/10/56	Pontypool Road Shops **U**
19/10/57	Pontypool Road Shops **U**
6/6/58	Swindon Works **HG**
26/11/59	Caerphilly Works **LC**
16/6/60	Hereford Shops **U**
24/10/60	Pontypool Road Shops **U**
7/12/60	Pontypool Road Shops **U**
21/4/61	Swindon Works **HI**
2/7/62	Pontypool Road Shops **U**
30/2/63	Ebbw Jct. Shops **U**
30/6/63	Pontypool Road Shops **U**
21/9/63	Swindon Works **HG**
22/6/64	Severn Tunnel Jct.
23/6/64	Hereford Shops **U**
7/11/64	Cardiff East Dock
7/8/65	Worcester

Tenders

From new	2130
2/4/42	1902
14/3/45	2904
30/10/47	2044
12/9/50	2265
19/5/52	2908
4/12/53	2244
6/6/58	2440
23/2/61	2812
21/4/61	2646
15/11/63	2251

Mileage at 28/12/63 834,900
Withdrawn 31/12/65

6872 CRAWLEY GRANGE against the mighty Old Oak Common coal stage, in August 1956. A Pontypool Road loco in London would probably have been a little unusual, though GW/WR locos did seem to roam more indiscriminately than many on other Railways/Regions. J. Robertson, transporttreasury

Pontypool Road's 6872 at the new Whiteball Siding box, 21 July 1956, hauling the 4.15pm Paignton-Paddington, load 12, working through. 6972 had come down the previous night on one of six 13 and 14 coach runners off the North & West to Paignton, starting at Huddersfield and Preston as well as Manchester. This amounted to 350-400 miles in 24 hours which was routine for a Grange; they did this most summer weekends, 3,500 gallon tenders notwithstanding. R.C. Riley, transporttreasury

6873 CARADOC GRANGE
Built April 1939

Mileages and Boilers
Date	Mileage	Boiler
From new		7263
18/2/42	95,585	7263
26/5/44	166,666	7263
25/5/46	225,016	C4043
10/6/47	263,009	C4043
7/6/49	331,78	C8252
13/11/50	379,39	C8284
6/6/52	448,204	C4037
9/8/54	547,809	C2948
8/1/57	662,710	C2948
9/2/59	753,035	C2957
3/11/61	855,782	C4947
1/11/63	908,451	C7246

Sheds and Works
29/4/39	Westbury
1/11/39	Westbury Shops **R**
12/12/39	Severn Tunnel Jct
12/9/40	Severn Tunnel Jct. Shops **R**
21/10/41	Severn Tunnel Jct. Shops **R**
18/2/42	Swindon Works **I**
26/5/44	Swindon Works **I**
10/4/45	Penzance Shops **R**
19/7/45	Severn Tunnel Shops **R**
25/5/46	Swindon Works **L**
10/6/47	Swindon Works **I**
18/1/48	Bath Road Shops **R**
15/5/48	Oxley
11/7/48	Oxley Shops **L**
7/6/49	Swindon Works **HG**
25/2/50	Laira
26/5/50	Taunton Shops **U**
13/11/50	Swindon Works **HC**
3/1/52	Laira Shops **U**
6/6/52	Swindon Works **HI**
14/6/53	Laira Shops **U**
2/10/53	Laira Shops **U**
10/6/54	Laira Shops **U**
9/8/54	Swindon Works **HG**
15/10/55	Laira Shops **U**
24/3/56	Newton Abbot Shed **U**
8/11/56	Laira Shops **U**
8/1/57	Swindon Works **I**
19/10/57	Newton Abbot Works **LC**
24/4/58	Laira Shops **U**
27/12/58	Penzance
21/1/59	Laira
9/2/59	Swindon Works **HG**
30/5/61	Laira Shops **U**
3/11/61	Swindon Works **HI**
16/3/62	Westbury Shops **U**
19/5/62	St. Philips Marsh
7/12/62	St. Philips Marsh Shops **U**
22/2/63	Southall Shops **U**
1/11/63	Wolverhampton Works **HC**
21/4/64	Worcester shops **U**

Tenders
Date	Tender
From new	2241
24/7/39	2328
18/2/42	2329
26/5/44	2005
25/5/46	2900
10/6/47	2921
7/6/49	2367
6/6/52	2265
9/8/54	2258
9/2/59	2265
3/11/61	2771

Mileage at 28/12/63 912,317
Withdrawn 15/6/64

6873 CARADOC GRANGE down among the diesels at Penzance shed at the end of steam in 1962. J. Leaf, ColourRail.

With 4,000 gallon tender, 6873 CARADOC GRANGE heads a goods near Church Stretton; the train is likely to be the 12.10pm Shrewsbury-Pontypool Road 'E' freight. The period is April 1963 and the engine bears an 82A Bristol Bath Road plate. There is no reason to doubt the date; it is clearly after 1957 (with the second emblem) but according to its record, 6873 was never allocated to Bath Road; indeed, by April 1963 the place had closed to steam and the loco was at St Philips Marsh. Moreover there is further photographic evidence of it with the 82A plate at Temple Meads on 25 May 1963. Were there a few 82A shedplates knocking about there, sent over from Bath Road with all the other spare material and it got put on in error? Norman Preedy Archive.

6874 HAUGHTON GRANGE
Built April 1939

Mileages and Boilers

From new		7264
25/5/42	107,468	7264
11/1/45	196,999	C2921
13/2/48	306,444	C4955
10/2/50	381,209	C4037
7/5/52	466,456	C7246
1/12/54	564,521	C4070
1/5/57	666,138	C2961
18/12/59	773,109	C6204
29/6/62	850,358	C2953

Sheds and Works

29/4/39	Weymouth
11/11/39	Ebbw Jct.
25/5/42	Swindon Works **I**
11/1/45	Swindon Works **HG**
2/8/46	Bath Road Shops **R**
13/2/47	Ebbw Jct. Shops **R**
29/3/47	Hereford Shops **R**
8/7/47	Ebbw Jct. Shed **R**
25/9/47	Ebbw Jct. Shed **R**
9/12/47	Ebbw Jct. Shops **L** Tender work only
13/2/48	Swindon Works **I**
13/8/48	Old Oak Shops **L** Tender Work only
29/10/49	Ebbw Jct. Shops **U**
10/2/50	Swindon Works **HG**
23/3/52	Old Oak
7/5/52	Swindon Works **HG**
1/11/52	Newton Abbot
3/10/53	Taunton
1/12/54	Swindon Works **HI**
16/4/56	Taunton Shops **U**
14/5/56	Newton Abbot **U**
1/5/57	Swindon Works **HG**
18/12/59	Swindon Works **HI**
1/3/61	Taunton Shops **U**
9/9/61	St. Philips Marsh
25/9/61	St. Philips Marsh Shops **U**
27/1/62	Penzance
16/2/62	Penzance Shops **U**
29/6/62	Swindon Works **HG**
14/7/62	Laira
6/10/62	Didcot
18/10/63	Old Oak Shops **U**
2/11/63	Oxford
19/8/64	Westbury Shops **U**

Tenders

From new	2103
14/9/40	2002
25/5/42	1759
13/2/48	2131
13/8/48	1716
10/2/50	2256
7/5/52	2670
1/12/54	2249
18/12/59	2719
29/6/62	2250

Mileage at 28/12/63 890,996
Withdrawn 10/9/65

HAUGHTON GRANGE at Taunton, 25 August 1959. Ken Fairey, ColourRail.

6874 HAUGHTON GRANGE on Dainton with a goods on 31 July 1957, not long after a Heavy General; lined green, 'intermediate' 3,500 gallon tender with second emblem. Ray Hinton Archive, courtesy Norman Preedy.

6875 HINDFORD GRANGE

Built April 1939

Mileages and Boilers

From new		7265
9/1/42	100,860	7265
27/7/44	185,994	C4469
15/4/47	279,694	C8202
5/8/49	354,866	C8261
16/5/52	449,786	C8223
20/8/54	538,820	C8204
14/2/57	635,447	C6222
14/4/59	731,843	C4991
28/2/62	818,166	C6220

Sheds and Works

29/4/39	Pontypool Road
9/1/42	Swindon Works **I**
2/10/43	Pontypool Road Shops **L**
9/2/44	Didcot Shops **R**
27/7/44	Swindon Works **HG**
15/4/47	Swindon Works **I**
16/6/47	Canton Shops **L**
5/8/49	Swindon Works **HG**
12/8/50	Taunton
25/2/51	Taunton Shops **U**
11/6/51	Taunton Shops **U**
7/11/51	Taunton Shops **U**
16/5/52	Swindon Works **HG**
7/4/53	Taunton Shops **U**
20/8/54	Swindon Works **HG**
4/3/55	Taunton Shops **U**
4/11/55	Taunton Shops **U**
16/12/55	Taunton Shops **U**
13/2/56	Taunton Shops **U**
6/6/56	Taunton Shops **U**
14/2/57	Swindon Works **HI**
28/12/57	Penzance
14/4/59	Swindon Works **HG**
7/5/60	Penzance Shops **U**
18/6/60	St Blazey
7/2/61	St. Blazey Shops **U**
11/10/61	St. Blazey Shops **U**
4/11/61	Penzance
28/2/62	Swindon Works **HI**
28/2/62	Penzance
6/10/62	Cardiff East Dock
3/4/63	Shrewsbury Shops **U**
29/6/63	Southall
24/2/64	St. Philips Marsh

Tenders

From new	2206
9/1/42	2241
27/7/44	2236
23/2/47	2164
16/6/47	2220
10/6/49	2873
5/8/49	2248
16/5/52	2859
20/8/54	2390
14/2/57	2787
14/4/59	2081
28/2/62	2610

Mileage at 28/12/63 864,114
Withdrawn 10/3/64, sold to R S Hayes, Bridgend, 23/4/64

6875 HINDFORD GRANGE newly outshopped and glistening in green (lined) at Swindon, April 1959. The later on in the Grange story, the more anachronistic the low-sided tenders seem. In hindsight of course; it meant not much at all at Swindon, awash with tenders; 6875 had had a 4,000 gallon tender not long before – see next for instance. B.K.B. Green Collection, Initial Photographics.

HINDFORD GRANGE (4,000 gallon tender, first emblem) at Exeter St David's, 28 July 1957. B.K.B. Green Collection, Initial Photographics.

6876 KINGSLAND GRANGE

Built April 1939

Mileages and Boilers

From new		7266
4/2/42	104,276	7266
16/11/44	194,878	C7216
10/11/47	298,162	C2845
24/2/50	386,838	C2939
6/10/52	487,451	C4474
20/6/55	585,710	C2976
20/2/58	682,198	C2976
4/8/60	769,151	C4993
6/11/63	847,727	6222

Sheds and Works

27/5/39	St. Philips Marsh
17/9/40	St. Philips Marsh Shops **R**
18/10/40	Swindon Works **L**
4/2/42	Swindon Works **I**
14/6/43	Newton Abbot Works **L**
16/11/44	Swindon Works **HG**
1/12/45	Exeter Shops **R**
28/11/46	St. Philips Marsh **R**
13/9/46	Westbury Shed **R**
9/10/46	Hereford Shops **R**
4/5/47	Bath Road Shops **L**
6/6/47	Bath Road Shops **L** Tender Work only
10/11/47	Swindon Works **I**
24/2/50	Swindon Works **HG**
14/9/50	Newton Abbot Shed **U**
10/1/52	Newton Abbot Works **U**
6/10/52	Swindon Works **HG**
2/6/53	St. Philips Marsh Shops **U**
13/8/54	Laira Shops **U**
20/6/55	Swindon Works **HG**
21/2/56	Bath Road Shops **U**
23/1/57	Old Oak Shops **U**
20/2/58	Swindon Works **HI**
9/10/58	St. Philips Marsh Shops **U**
18/4/59	Ebbw Jct.
4/8/60	Swindon Works **HG**
4/11/61	Pontypool Road
28/1/62	Hereford Shops **U**
28/2/62	Hereford Shops **U**
26/4/62	Hereford Shops **U**
12/9/62	Hereford Shops **U**
19/10/62	Pontypool Road Shops **U**
6/11/63	Swindon Works **HI**
22/6/64	Severn Tunnel Jct.
2/7/64	Worcester Shops **U**
9/1/65	Ebbw Jct.
6/3/65	Cardiff East Dock
7/8/65	Ebbw Jct.
6/11/65	Worcester

Tenders

From new	2210
18/10/40	1744
10/11/47	2030
24/2/50	1916
6/10/52	2907
20/6/55	2699
3/1057	2434
20/2/58	2355
4/8/60	2540
6/11/63	2246

Mileage at 28/12/63 852,151
Withdrawn 18/11/65

Scruffy at Gloucester, 12 October 1964. J.L. Stevenson, courtesy Hamish Stevenson.

Ex-works in plain black, June 1955.

6877 LLANFAIR GRANGE

Built April 1939

Mileages and Boilers

From new		7267
31/7/42	115,201	7267
29/6/45	212,957	C4463
8/12/47	303,787	C2816
19/5/50	404,015	C4421
30/7/52	494,552	C8259
15/12/54	591,716	C9288
9/4/57	676,321	C7275
24/6/58	721,480	C4413
23/6/60	791,633	C4413
12/9/62	855,595	C2954

Sheds and Works

27/5/39	Worcester
3/742	Swindon Works **I**
11/9/42	Reading Shops **R**
15/3/44	Worcester Shops **L**
29/6/45	Swindon Works **HG**
1/4/46	Worcester Shops **R**
25/3/47	Worcester Shops **R**
8/12/47	Swindon Works **I**
15/7/49	Worcester Shops **U**
19/5/50	Swindon Works **HG**
30/7/52	Swindon Works **HG**
15/12/54	Swindon Works **HG**
23/6/56	Worcester Shops **U**
18/10/56	Worcester Shops **U**
9/4/57	Swindon Works **HI**
24/6/58	Swindon Works **HC**
23/6/60	Wolverhampton Works **HI**
26/7/60	Tyseley Shops **U**
26/10/61	Worcester Shops **U**
4/5/62	Worcester Shops **U**
12/9/62	Swindon Works **HG**
10/10/62	Worcester Shops **U**
16/7/63	Worcester Shops **U**
29/6/64	Worcester Shops **U**

Tenders

From new	1904
3/7/42	2888
29/6/45	2599
9/12/47	2241
19/5/50	2254
20/9/50	1639
13/6/52	2668
9/8/54	2253
15/12/54	2256
9/4/57	2440
24/6/58	2543
27/11/58	2569
12/9/62	2264

Mileage at 28/12/63 889,356
Withdrawn 3/1965

6877 LLANFAIR GRANGE at Wolverhampton Low Level, 1957. It has been said that 'Llanfair' was the proper Welsh rendering, 6825's 'Llanvair' the English one – two names for the same place; it has also been said that they are in fact two separate locations... Michael Boakes Collection.

LLANFAIR GRANGE at Exeter St David's on the uncomfortably crowded 8.50am Swansea-Paignton train, 26 July 1958, in the days when people looked out of trains and people looked at trains too! 'What's the hold up?' seems to be on everyone's lips. As it turns out, the time is 2.43pm and with the whole westbound service, Western and Southern, running 50-60 minutes late, not all the comments from the carriage windows may have been complimentary. B.W.L. Brooksbank, Initial Photographics.

6878 LONGFORD GRANGE

Built May 1939

Mileages and Boilers

From new		7268
22/11/41	91,127	7268
12/2/44	164,043	7268
10/2/45	196,315	C4021
19/8/46	248,565	C2910
17/11/49	338,744	C7230
25/1/52	408,529	C7230
28/5/54	497,250	C7221
4/4/57	569,911	C4937
18/2/60	656,432	C2834
5/9/62	735,933	C7210

Sheds and Works

27/5/39	Oxley
22/11/41	Wolverhampton Works I
2/2/42	Stafford Road Shed R
26/5/42	Stafford Road Shed R
12/2/44	Swindon Works I
5/5/44	Stafford Road Shed L
10/2/45	Swindon Works L
19/8/46	Swindon Works HG
30/11/46	Birkenhead*
20/11/47	Birkenhead Shops L
	Tender Work only
11/12/47	Old Oak Shops I
15/2/48	Birkenhead Shops R
26/4/48	Birkenhead Shops R
22/12/48	Wolverhampton Works L
12/8/49	Birkenhead Shops U
17/11/49	Swindon Works HG
14/8/51	Birkenhead Shops U
25/1/52	Swindon Works HI
20/3/52	Birkenhead Shops U
24/8/52	Birkenhead Shops U
28/5/54	Swindon Works HG
22/3/56	Birkenhead Shops U
10/8/56	Tyseley Shops U
4/4/57	Swindon Works HI
18/9/57	Birkenhead Shops U
14/6/58	St. Philips Marsh
15/1/59	Caerphilly Works U
25/3/59	St. Philips Marsh shops U
30/7/59	Neath Shops U
18/2/60	Swindon Works HG
2/4/61	St. Philips Marsh Shops U
6/5/62	St. Philips Marsh Shops U
5/9/62	Swindon Works HI
13/4/64	Llanelly
4/5/64	Ebbw Jct.
22/6/64	Worcester

Birkenhead GW later incorporated into LMR shed as 6C

Tenders

From new	1876
12/244	2004
10/2/45	2902
19/8/46	2325
8/1/47	2888
17/11/49	2104
28/5/54	2932
4/4/57	2860
18/2/60	2681
5/9/62	4015*

Late built Collett tender of 1946.

Mileage at 28/12/63 780,650
Withdrawn 27/11/64

6878 LONGFORD GRANGE, nominally an LMR locomotive (allocated to 6C Birkenhead) at Wrexham on 21 July 1951; Churchward tender 2104. R.C. Riley, transporttreasury

LONGFORD GRANGE at Chester shed, now with second emblem 4,000 gallon tender. It is about 1957-58, just before it moved to St Philips Marsh. A. Robey, transporttreasury

6879 OVERTON GRANGE
Built May 1939

Sheds and Works
27/5/39	Oxley
8/1941	Wolverhampton Works
23/2/43	Swindon Works **HG**
5/1943	Swindon Works
1/10/45	Wolverhampton Works **I**
17/5/47	Swindon Works
25/8/48	Swindon Works **I**
30/3/51	Swindon Works **HI**
19/4/52	Banbury
4/10/52	Oxley
21/1/53	Swindon Works **HI**
6/11/54	Swindon Works **HG**
25/3/55	Oxley Shops **LC**
2/2/56	Swindon Works **LC**
14/12/56	Wolverhampton Works **LC**
30/3/57	Swindon Works **HG**
14/6/58	Laira
27/12/58	Truro
11/7/59	St. Blazey
18/11/59	Stourbridge
28/3/60	Swindon Works **HI**
23/4/60	Tyseley
30/8/62	Swindon Works **HG**

Tenders
From new	2027
1940	2247
1944	2921
1948	2261 [27/9/48]
1952	2923
1954	2906 2252 [29/11/55]
1956	2872
1958	2932
1960	2255 [28/3/60]
1962	2832

NO FURTHER DETAIL

Withdrawn 16/10/65

6879 OVERTON GRANGE by the shore at Shaldon Bridge, Teignmouth with empty stock, August 1957. The grime is too thick see the lined green or to determine tender emblem but the loco still has the taper buffers. J. Robertson, transporttreasury

The last of the Granges, 6879 OVERTON GRANGE, now of Tyseley passes eastwards between the two tunnels at Chester on a down express off the WR, about 1961. The loco is in excellent condition and tows a 4,000 gallon tender, 'which always seemed to suit these locos better than the lower 'Victorian' ones' as someone once said. RailOnline.

On a parcels at Bristol Temple Meads, 29 September 1956. D.M. Alexander, transporttreasury

Endpiece

6854 ROUNDHILL GRANGE at Paddington in July 1954. It would have been one of the few Granges to be seen regularly at Paddington. From new until 1959 it was operating from Banbury, Oxford and Oxley on such passenger duties as this: semi-fasts to and from Oxford and the West Midlands. B.H. Fletcher, transporttreasury